A Western Horseman Book
Colorado Springs, Colorado

TEAM ROPING

By Leo Camarillo

with Randy Witte

Photographs by Kurt Markus

TEAM ROPING

Published by
The Western Horseman, Inc.
3850 North Nevada Avenue
Colorado Springs, Colorado 80933

Typography
McNamara Publishing
Conifer, Colorado

Printing
Williams Printing
Colorado Springs, Colorado

Design
Kurt Markus

Manufactured in the United States of America
ISBN 0-911647-00-7

DEDICATION

I dedicate this book to the men and women in all
careers who know what it's like to have paid the price of
dedication and self-discipline in striving to achieve the
rewards that come along in their pursuit of perfection.

Leo Camarillo

LEO CAMARILLO

CONTENTS

Right- and left-handed ropers

6 PREFACE

Roping times are faster because of the Camarillo influence

8 INTRODUCTION

Use whatever you have as long as it's functional and serviceable

10 EQUIPMENT

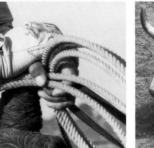

Ropes, Dummies, Horses & Gear

"I like to think of the header as the quarterback"

18 HEADING

From the Ground   From the Horse

"The heeler is the wide receiver of the team"

50 HEELING

From the Ground   From the Horse

76 ACTION

Sequence pictures of several runs

114 HORSES

A good roper on the ground is not necessarily a good roper from the back of a horse

Horsemanship, Training, Care & Conditioning, Practicing

124 CATTLE

Care and the Corriente

126 PROFILE

Leo Camarillo: the man, the athlete -- "Roping is what I do"

The Lion at Large

140 RULES

Synopsis from the PRCA book

142 TERMINOLOGY

Team roping lingo

PREFACE

The diagram shows the difference in positioning for left-handed heelers, as compared to right-handed heelers.

This book is written mainly for right-handed ropers, simply because most people are right-handed. But southpaw ropers should be able to interpret the instructions to fit their needs; for example, when we talk about dallying the rope around the saddle horn in a counter-clockwise motion, left-handers will know they should dally in a clockwise motion. Left-handed ropers can head a steer as well as a right-handed person, but usually choose to heel, instead.

There is a reason for this: at most rodeos or ropings, the barrier rope is stretched in front of the left-hand box, and the header is the one who must start from behind the barrier. A left-handed header would have to rope the steer and lead him off to the right of the arena, rather than the left, and this would force the heeler to cross over behind the header in order to make his catch—an awkward procedure. So, most southpaw team ropers are heelers. The diagrams below show the differences in positioning for left-handed

heelers, as compared to right-handed heelers.

Even if a person knows he wants to take up heeling at the outset, it would probably be best to read the book from the beginning, including the section on heading. Basic rope handling techniques are explained fully in the heading section, and only touched on in heeling in order to avoid too much repetition.

Left-handers can use a right-hander's rope by simply reversing the coils and loop. Hold the coiled rope in your right hand, pass the loop through the middle of the coils to your left hand, then re-coil the rest of the rope so that the tail comes out of the top of the hand holding the coils, rather than the bottom. This will allow the rope to stay in its natural twist. Rope that is twisted in the opposite direction of the standard rope is also available for left-handed ropers.

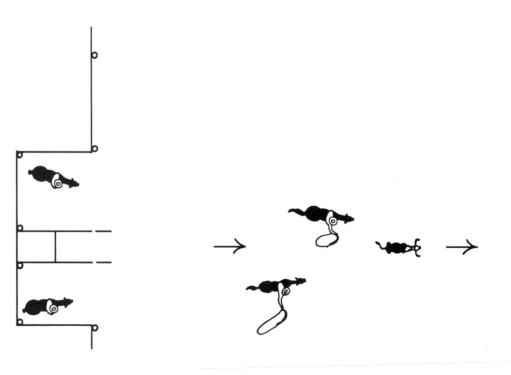

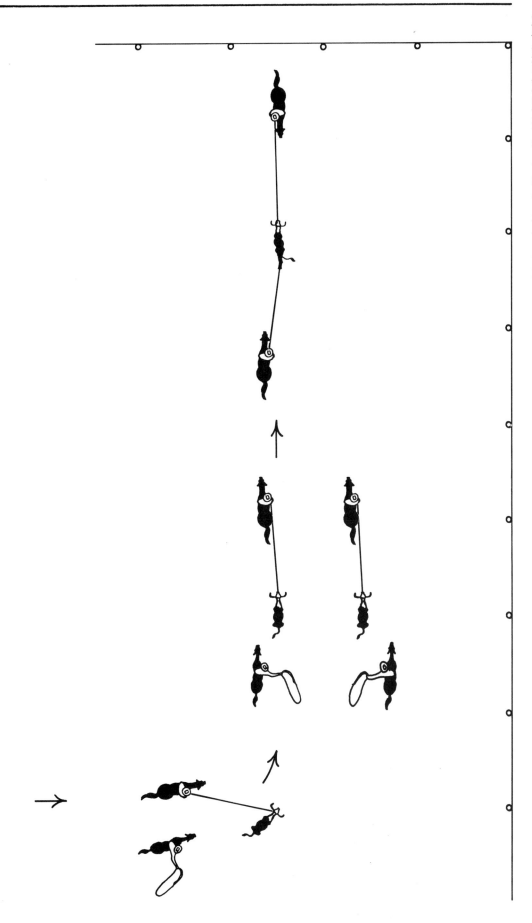

A right-handed heeler will position himself behind the steer's left hip. A left-hander will rope from behind the steer's right hip. A team roping run is complete when both ropers face one another with ropes taut and steer in the middle.

Introduction

"Learn the basics correctly, and then practice, practice, practice."

Leo Camarillo.

Team roping, one of the oldest events in rodeo, simply evolved from an efficient method of handling livestock on open range. For that matter, the practice of heading and heeling cattle, temporarily immobilizing them between two ropes for doctoring, branding, or whatever the need may be, is still used on many ranches in the course of a day's work. Naturally, the cowboys speeded it up for the arena to make a game of it, just as they made a sport of saddle bronc riding, another contest born of necessity.

But of all rodeo events, team roping is the only one that can be practiced and enjoyed by adults and children of nearly all ages. It's like golf, in a way—there are professional ropers, but there are also many who enjoy the game on their own levels, as a hobby with friends and neighbors, practicing and competing at roping arenas around the country.

This book is for beginners, for those who want to learn the basics of team roping. But even more advanced ropers will likely pick up a few tips on roping and horsemanship from Leo Camarillo.

No other name in the history of rodeo is more synonymous with team roping than Camarillo. Leo, with his younger brother Jerold and cousin Reg Camarillo, forged a roping dynasty that began in 1968 and revolutionized the event. Reg, semi-retired from the game and now a full-time horse trainer, is still recognized as one of the greatest headers. Jerold, 1969 world champion team roper, continues to be the heeler to beat at any roping, and he qualifies each year for the National Finals.

As for Leo, it's easy to begin a rundown of his accomplishments, but hard to find a place to quit—and the story is ongoing. Leo continues to dominate his event as a heeler like no one before him. And he is recognized as one of the best all-around ropers because he is equally adept at heading, and has

shown further versatility as a calf roper, single steer roper, and even as a steer wrestler.

Beyond that, it is Leo's style of heeling, which he pioneered, that revolutionized team roping. Leo and Jerold hit the pros with a bang, roping heels out of the air rather than throwing the traditional heel loop that hits the ground in front of the hind legs. No other style of heeling has been more widely copied in recent years. Dave Stout, the noted rodeo writer and historian, a roper and past secretary-treasurer of the PRCA, lends credence to this statement.

"Before the Camarillos came into professional team roping, the event was mainly a contest for older rodeo hands," Stout said. "There were exceptions, of course, like Jim Rodriguez, who won his first team roping championship at age 18 in 1959. And I won't say absolutely that no one had ever roped any heels out of the air before Leo and Jerold did when they joined the association in 1968. But the fact is, the Camarillos made such an impression on everyone with that winning style of heeling that other ropers started trying it in an effort to beat them. And a lot of young, athletic ropers were lured into the event after watching the Camarillos win. Team roping times are much faster in rodeo today because of the Camarillo influence; there's no doubt about that."

Leo explains in the book what this speedy catch entails, but he teaches beginners the traditional heel catch. "You've got to learn to walk before you run," he says. He and Jerold and Reg have held roping clinics throughout the country, teaching the basics to aspiring team ropers. And Leo acknowledges that such schools gradually result in stiffer competition in professional rodeo, but he is candid and confident about his own ability: "They've still got to beat *me*." Besides, he views the growing popularity of the event as a healthy trend—financially healthy for professionals, and healthy from a recreational standpoint for everyone else.

Whatever level of competition or recreation a beginner strives for, he may as well learn from the best. The instructor's credentials are impressive. With the assistance of various partners through the years, Leo has won the team roping average at the National Finals more than anyone. His wins came in 1968 through 1971, and again in 1980. He was world champion team roper in 1972, 1973, and 1975, the year he also won the Professional Rodeo Cowboys Association world all-around championship. He was team roping champ for the regular season in 1976 (during a three-year interim in which the PRCA named world champions solely on the basis of winnings at the National Finals).

Leo sacrificed his chance for another title in 1980 by heeling for his rookie partner Tee Woolman, who went into the Finals only a few dollars ahead of Leo. The pair put on a roping demonstration that will long be remembered, winning five of ten go-rounds, including three with consecutive times of 5.4 seconds. They won the Finals, accumulating a record number of points under the Finals scoring system, and Tee gained his first gold buckle. The week after the '80 Finals, Leo and Tee went to a rodeo in Las Vegas, Nevada. They roped a steer in 4.8 seconds, a record fast time that, at this writing, still stands.

Money aside, Leo really doesn't need more championships to assure his niche in team roping annals. His competitors respect him, his students watch and learn from him. Now read what he has to say about the sport and follow his advice: "Learn the basics correctly, and then practice, practice, practice."

— Randy Witte

Randy Witte.

Leo and his cousin Reg Camarillo, one of the best headers of all time. The two roped together to provide the demonstration photos for this book.

9

EQUIPMENT

ROPES

I always pack a variety of ropes with me, ranging from hard to soft, from "nearly brand new" to "almost worn out."

First thing you'll need is a good nylon rope — one that feels good to you, that you're comfortable working with. The only way you'll discover which size and type of rope feels best is to gradually try a variety of ropes. There are two popular diameters of rope, 3/8ths (smaller and lighter) and 7/16ths (larger and heavier). And each diameter comes in a variety of "lays" (the stiffness factor) that range from soft to hard.

For beginners, especially youngsters, I suggest you start with the 3/8ths category in the medium lay area for heeling; minimum length should be 35 feet. For heading, you'll want a little heavier rope — try a 7/16ths soft or medium with a minimum length of 30 feet.

I've always used mediums; they feel good to me. And that's what I want in my rope — the feel and confidence that I can handle it effectively. After you've roped long enough to develop this feel, you may want to change to a softer or harder rope, whichever feels best to you. When I get a new rope, I take one that feels just a little stiffer than I like; after I've used that rope awhile, and it's "broke in," the natural feel will be a little softer than what it was hanging in the store. Also, a new rope should have the honda tied so it twists slightly to the right. You want the honda to lay straight, but if it's initially tied straight, it will probably end up twisting to the left after it's broke in. To check the honda, hold the rope in front of you with the "burner" facing away.

One thing you should be aware of is that weather conditions can really affect how much body or life a rope has (the way a nylon rope feels and handles). Cool weather makes a nylon rope softer; hot weather makes it stiffer. The nylon contracts or expands, depending on the temperature. For this reason, I always pack a variety of ropes with me, ranging from hard to soft, from "nearly brand new" to "almost worn out." That way, no matter what the weather is like, I can reach in my rope bag and find a rope that has the particular feel I want.

DUMMIES

Once you've got a rope, you're ready to start working out on a practice dummy. You can purchase a variety of dummies, or you can make your own (like those in the accompanying photos) — use your imagination. A sawhorse works fine for heeling practice; put some kind of head and horns on the front and you can use it for heading practice as well. Another popular heading dummy consists of a bale of hay with a set of horns (or something resembling horns) stuck in the front of the bale. A lot of saddle shops, feed stores, and western wear stores have dummy heads and horns available just for this purpose.

You'll probably spend a lot more

My favorite heading dummy, "at rest" in the tack room.

10

A heeling dummy (left) and heading dummy.

time with the practice dummy than you will actually roping steers. I used to really work a dummy — I'd pick out certain shots I wanted to perfect, as if I were out of position, and I'd practice until I could make the rope do exactly what I wanted it to do no matter where I was standing. This is called ground work, and I can't emphasize enough how important it is. We'll get back to the dummy when we discuss the specifics of heading and heeling.

HORSES AND GEAR

A beginner needs a horse that knows more about team roping than he does. Whether you own such a horse, or have access to one, you've got to be mounted on something you can handle that knows what team roping is about. For most beginners, this means acquiring an experienced roping horse — a horse that maybe isn't as fast as he used to be, but is solid. A horse like

Quarter Horses are ideal for team roping and other rodeo events. This one, Shorty, is one of my heel horses.

11

The saddle horn is a handy place to store your horse's bell boots when they're not in use.

this can teach you something; hang around other ropers and roping arenas, and you'll find horses for sale. Have an experienced, knowledgeable friend help you make a choice.

For those who are already roping with a fair degree of consistency, we'll discuss the basic training and make-up of rope horses in one of the following chapters.

As for saddles and bridles, use whatever you have as long as they are functional and fit the horse. My favorite bit, incidentally, is a hackamore bit; I get all the response I want with it, and it isn't a severe bit. I can save my horse's mouth, and my horse works in it. However, this bit will not work on

Here's a close-up of the headgear I use on Stick, my favorite heeling horse.

The latigo, wrapped up and out of the way for unsaddling.

all horses.

Roping reins are better than split reins because they won't get tangled in the coils of rope you're holding in the same hand with the reins. This equipment doesn't have to be fancy or expensive, but it should be sturdy and safe. Your saddle should have some type of a double rigging, one with a front and back cinch that are both fairly wide to distribute the pressure more evenly when you cinch up tight. And the saddle should be strong enough to take the jerks when you rope a steer. The saddle horn should be high enough to take a couple of wraps around it with your rope when you dally, and it shouldn't slope too far forward, or have an exceptionally large or small cap (the top part of the horn).

I should point out that any time you have quality equipment that fits you and your horse perfectly, it pays off in the long run. The saddle I ride has a rawhide-covered wood tree and extra heavy rigging, a "two-rope" post horn with a 2 3/4-inch cap, 13-inch swell, 3-inch oval cantle, 3-inch deep raw-

You'll need to wrap your saddle horn with strips of old innertube to protect it from wear caused by dallying. The innertube strips, figure-eighted over the horn, also help hold a dallied rope. This is the ideal thickness of rubber around the horn. Some ropers put on too much; others don't use enough.

*Check your equipment
frequently. Look for
signs of wear.*

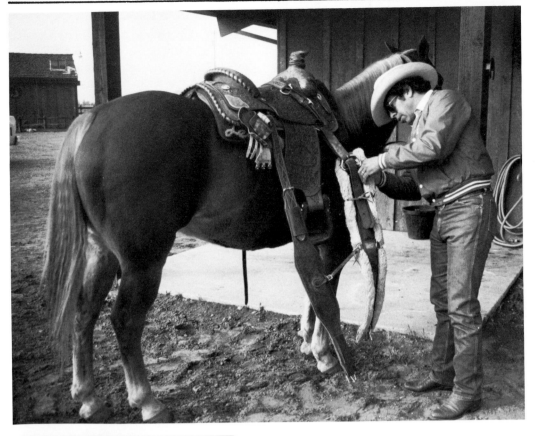

*I like an extra-wide "roper girth" with padding
extending over the cinch rings. This cinch won't
gall a horse.*

*A handy place to store splint boots when not in
use--buckled to a small ring at the back of the
saddle.*

14

hide-covered roper stirrups, extra-wide roper girth, 5-inch heavy doubled and stitched flank cinch, and stainless steel dee rings in front and back. Total weight is 48 pounds.

Professional ropers are extremely particular about their equipment, and a saddle that fits one person may not feel completely comfortable to another. For example, Dee Pickett has a saddle that is similar to mine but not exactly like it. I don't like Dee's saddle as well as mine; he likes his saddle better than mine. But a beginner would probably do equally well in either saddle.

Other horse gear you'll need includes

Breast collar attached to saddle rigging.

Rawhide-covered roper stirrup.

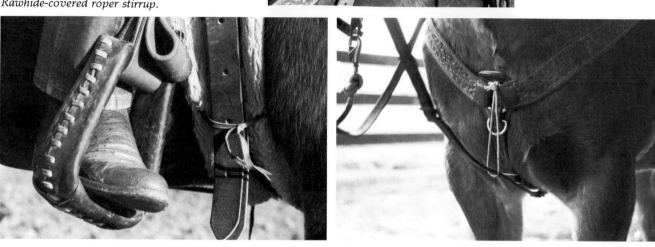

Tie-down strap (passing through the keeper), and breast collar, all attached to the small cinch ring under the horse. Notice how the breast collar dips down in the middle--this type of collar won't choke a heading horse when he starts pulling a steer on the end of a rope.

The tie-down adjustment will vary among horses. This shows how I have it adjusted on Stick. One word of caution: if you put a tie-down on a horse that has never had one on before, let him get used to it on his own, without a rider. Some horses will panic and try to rear the first time they feel a tie-down.

It takes only a minute to slip on rubber bell boots, and the protection this gives a horse is sure worth the time.

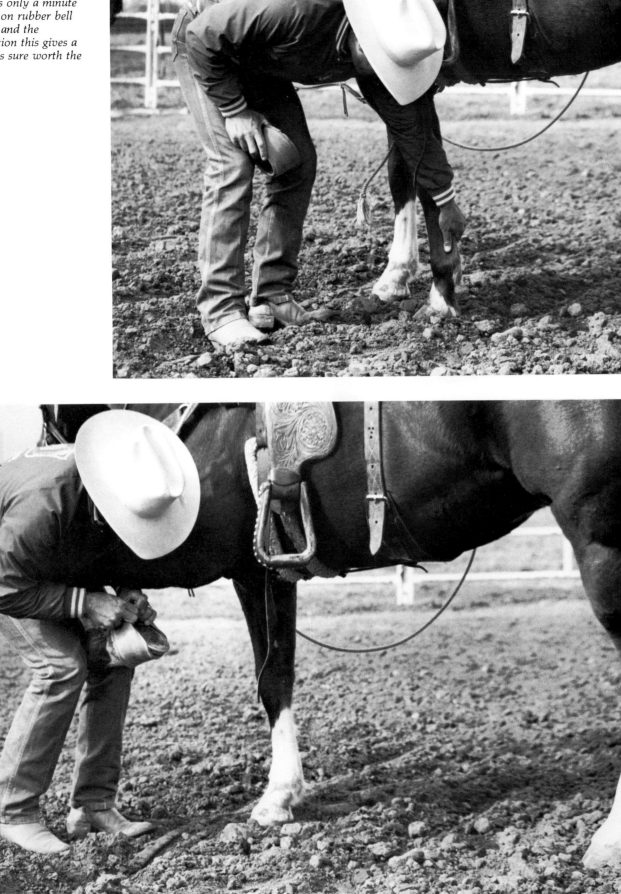

You can give yourself a little protection, too--from wear on your hand--if you use a special "roper's glove," available from many rodeo and roping suppliers.

a breast collar to help keep the saddle in place. This is essential for headers, optional for heelers, but I use a breast collar all the time, heading or heeling. I also like to use a tie-down for a little better control of the horse's head, and to help him use it as a brace to maintain his balance in certain situations. And I use over-reach boots and splint boots for the horse's front feet and legs. I rarely ride one of my horses without this last bit of protection. A horse can slip or over-reach with a hind foot, cutting one of his front feet or legs, and you'll be without a horse until the wound heals—unless you've taken steps to prevent that type of injury from occurring.

It's also a good idea to take a close look at all your equipment on a regular basis. Look for signs of wear on cinches, tie-down and breast collar straps, billets on the saddle. Replace things like these before they break. Check the leather burner on your rope; if it's about to wear through, you might end up with a worn-out honda, so put on a new burner. Keep your equipment in good working order.

Now, let's go over to the roping dummy.

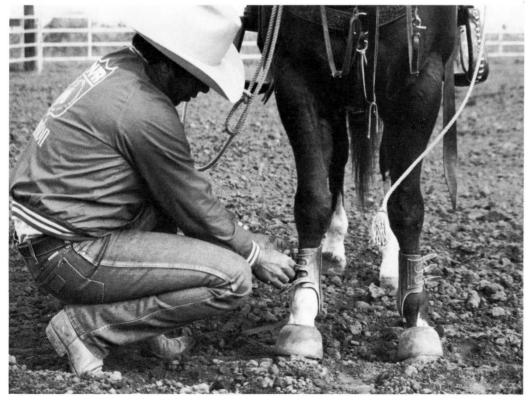

Placing splint boots on a horse's front legs gives added protection from injury caused by over-reaching with a hind foot, or by one front foot striking the opposite leg.

H E A D I N G

From the Ground

Let's begin by building a loop.

Position yourself behind the dummy where you would be if you were horseback, roping a real steer. That place is directly behind the steer's left hip. Hold the coils in your left hand and build a loop; you can flip the loop over in a clockwise fashion a time or two to the side as you build it to keep the rope from twisting. Study the accompanying photographs and learn how to hold the loop and coils correctly.

Notice how much spoke I have in the loop. I use a little longer spoke when roping horns than I would roping calves or polled cattle. The longer spoke keeps the loop flat as it hits the back of the steer's head and continues in a sideways motion from right to left.

1/

2/

Separate the small loop from the coils (1), then build the loop by rolling it backwards over your hand (2), and slipping your wrist inside to support it (3). Feed the coils one at a time until you get the loop the size you want it. Then hold the loop and coils properly (4), and you're ready to rope.

3/

4/

18

This is the size of loop I like to start with. Notice the length of the spoke: the distance between the honda and my hand. Beginning ropers probably won't want this much spoke to start with, because it's a little harder to swing the rope with a lot of spoke, but this is the length a beginner should strive for as he learns. I also like to leave quite a bit of tail hanging down from my left hand; this gives me fewer coils to hold, reducing the bulk in my left hand (a personal preference).

A short spoke will cause a loop to dip downward and to the side, which is what a calf roper wants. Although full head catches (around the steer's neck) and half-head catches (around the neck and one horn) are legal, the steer will move more erratically with these — he'll fight the rope — and the header won't be able to control him as well for the heeler to make his catch.

Begin by swinging the loop overhead, parallel to the ground. Get a lot of action in your wrist, and remember to keep your elbow up while swinging the loop. By that I don't mean simply holding your arm in the air — "keeping your elbow up" is probably the most misunderstood term in roping. Your elbow should be *twisted upwards* when your thumb is down as the loop moves in front of you. This helps keep the loop open and provides for a correct, consistent delivery of the loop.

Use your whole arm to throw, not just your wrist. When you release the rope, follow through with your arm and fingers pointing where you want that loop to go. The loop should move in a downward, crossing pattern to the horns; the honda should hit the steer on the back of the head between his horns. The loop will grab the right horn, and the momentum of the swing should carry the loop sideways over the left horn, and then swing in an upward figure-eight behind the left horn. *Right then*, when the loop has curled into the figure-eight, is when you want to reach down with your right hand and grab the slack. If you wait too long, that rope will settle back down over the steer's head; it may even drop

1/ *Begin by swinging the loop overhead.*

2/ *Look at your target.*

3/ *Use a strong, smooth, forceful throw, and follow through with your whole arm.*

4/ *As soon as the loop has encircled both horns and begins to figure-eight in an upward curling motion behind the left horn, reach for your slack and pull it.*

5/ *Use a strong, downward pull.*

1/ *Swinging the loop (photo sequence left to right, top to bottom): Look at my elbow--it rotates upwards with each swing.*

2/ *The elbow begins to rotate as the loop moves in front. The index finger is extended naturally for greater control.*

3/ *The arm rolls with the loop, keeping the loop open.*

4/ *You can see how the loop is rolling by comparing the position of the honda in the photo at left with the position of the honda in this photo, when the loop is moving behind me.*

5/A smooth release
with follow-through.

down lower and you'll get a front foot
in the loop (illegal catch). Incidentally,
a rope thrown with a little too much
authority may cause the figure-eight to
double back over the right horn (also
illegal).

When you grab the slack, your arm
is already extended because you've
followed through with your throw. Just
reach down and grab the rope between
your thumb and forefinger, palm
down, and let the rest of your fingers
curl around the rope as you pull all the
slack out of the rope, straight down,
not to the side. Pulling slack to the side
may cause the loop to "wave off" those
horns, especially on cattle with small
horns.

Usually, you'll take just one pull on
the slack, and that's all you have time
for anyway at most rodeos where
you're trying to dally as fast as you can
so the heeler can take his throw.
Sometimes though, especially at big
ropings where there are maybe five or
eight go-rounds and an average to
think about, good headers will pull

6/Ready to pull the
slack--my right hand is
starting to curl around
the rope, and my left
hand has a firm grip on
the rope. The rope will
slip through my right
hand as I pull
downward.

23

1/ *Here's another view of the swing and throw. Notice how the loop (photo at upper right) dips in front as it moves around my left side; this is proper. The loop should be delivered in a fairly flat, downward plane to the horns (right).*

2/

3/

4/

that slack a couple of times just to make sure the catch is extra tight and there is no way the loop will somehow slip off.

You'll spend a lot of time at the practice dummy before you get consistent with your catches, so don't get discouraged. Your goal is to develop a forceful, fluid throw; think of the rope as an extension of your arm.

We'll discuss dallying later, when we're horseback. Right now there is another aspect of rope handling I'd like to mention, and that is what we call "feeding the loop." Most good ropers feed their loops while they're swinging; all this means is you start with a loop that's a little smaller than the size of loop you want to have when you actually throw. You do this by gradually letting a coil slip out of your hand

5/ This loop was thrown with a lot of authority-- you can see how it is curling (upper left) and moving toward the (dummy's) right horn. If a loop is thrown too hard and you don't pull your slack fast enough, the figure-eight may accidentally catch the right horn again for an illegal catch. That didn't happen here.

1/ *The honda has hit its mark, behind the horns; the horns are encircled and the loop is swinging to the dummy's left side.*

2/ *The figure-eight forms (above), and the loop is pulled snugly around the horns (right).*

while you let the loop slip through your other hand a *little* with each swing. Centrifugal force created by swinging the loop pulls more rope into the loop.

You build the loop to whatever size you want according to conditions and according to when the loop feels comfortable to throw. If you really have to "reach" for a hard-running steer, you'll need a fairly large loop; if you are close to a steer, a smaller loop is best. You'll need a large loop for roping big, wide horns; you'll want a smaller loop for polled cattle, or cattle with smaller horns. Learn to adjust the loop to fit the target.

If you have a problem with your loop figure-eighting while you're swinging, you may be trying to feed the loop too fast, or you may be trying to go from a loop that's too small to a loop that's too big. Sometimes stiffer ropes also have a tendency to figure-eight in

the loop while you're swinging. You can avoid this before you rope by first flipping the loop over, thereby turning the length of rope over between your hands (see the photos on this).

Not everyone who ropes feeds the loop, but the best ropers do it. I do it because I have greater feel and control over the loop; I'm constantly working with my rope in this manner, rather than swinging a dead loop. In fact, when I'm roping, from the time I pick up my rope and begin swinging until I've actually finished with the dally, there is rope running through my hands almost constantly. The rope works for me like an extension of my body, not as an inanimate object. So, practice feeding the loop as you swing it; after four or five swings, or as soon as you feel the loop is the size you want, throw it.

Let's get our horses now and head some real steers.

26

Do you have a problem with a figure-eight forming in the loop as you build it? Look at the following photos for a quick remedy.

1/ *This loop has a figure-eight in it.*

2/Simply flip the loop backwards…

3/… over your arm…

4/… so it looks like this. Then…

5/... hold the loop in that position with your left hand for a moment while you grab the rope properly again with your right. The figure-eight is gone.

FROM THE HORSE

A horse can sense when his rider is nervous, so relax.

I like to think of the header as the quarterback of the team. He has to put the play in motion; he sets up the run. The steer must have a head start — that's what the barrier rope is for (not shown in these photos at my practice arena). When the header backs into that box, he should pick out a spot he wants the steer to reach when the gate is opened. This isn't necessarily a spot on the ground in front of the chute — the spot will vary with individuals. It may be a spot on the steer or the corner post.

A header will consider ground conditions, length of scoreline, even the cattle, and decide how far to let that steer move before he signals his horse to start so he won't break the barrier, and still won't be late leaving the box. He may decide to let the steer's shoulder get to the gate before he signals his horse, or halfway to the gate. Or, roping over a long scoreline, he may pick out a spot on the steer's hip, and decide to wait until the hip gets to the gate or

the corner post or whatever before he signals the horse. You want to "crowd" the barrier, but not break it, and thus avoid a ten-second penalty added to your time.

Gauging how far to let a steer move comes with experience. One thing that helps, if you're not first in line to rope, is to watch the other steers and ropers ahead of you.

Be relaxed and confident when you back your horse in the box. A horse can sense if his rider is nervous, and then he starts getting nervous. Just ride in, turn and back, and get ready to nod for the steer as soon as he's standing squarely in the chute, looking straight ahead. Remember, you want that steer to get a good clean break, too. If his head is turned or he's fighting the chute momentarily, he's liable to catch a horn or stumble for an instant when the gate is opened, and that makes for a bad start — you may break the barrier.

Your horse should be paying atten-

Be confident when you back your horse in the box. I happen to be in the heeler's box in this photo, but the same attitude should be assumed by the header.

Hold the reins in your left hand. Then put the coils of rope in your hand, on top of the reins.

tion, watching the steer, and standing squarely in the back of the box — *but not leaning against the back rail.* I see too many horses bracing themselves against the back of the box, like they're using that as a crutch. A horse standing like that can't break into a run as quickly as one that is standing squarely, in my opinion.

Advanced ropers may like to just hold the loop out to the side; others like to tuck it under their arm as they get ready for the run. I like to tuck the rope, especially for heading, and grab the saddle horn with my right hand. I think by doing this the roper will have a little better balance, and will be able to really get with the horse's motion as he leaves the box. You'll be able to pick up your rope and swing just as quickly as you could have by holding it out to the side.

I do hold the rope to the side quite often when I'm heeling. And I don't need to grab the saddle horn all the

Get off to a good balanced start by holding the saddle horn.

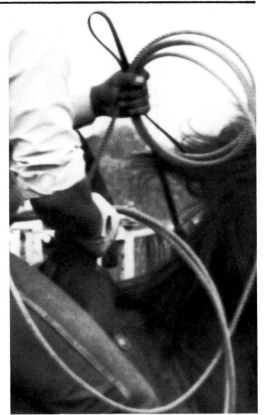

Beginning headers should move up to the steer's left hip and let the horse rate the steer.

time. Anyone who rides effectively and can get with the horse's motion immediately can do this. Also, in heeling, you've got just a little more time initially than the header does, so the start isn't quite as critical. But I tell all beginners to tuck that rope and hold onto the saddle horn—every time.

Once you've nodded for the steer and the gate flies open and the steer moves to that pre-determined spot, get to him as fast as you can. Beginners will want to run up to that steer's left hip, and then let the horse "rate" the steer—that is, pull up just a little so the horse and steer are running at the same speed while you're swinging your loop. A well-trained horse will do this automatically.

It's hard to rope cattle "coming to them," but of course this is what the better ropers have to do quite often to win. And some headers are good at throwing a long loop at cattle that are really running away. Just remember that in order to win, you first have to catch. The easiest way to make your head catch is when the horse is rating the steer.

Also, learn to ride the stirrups. Find

Learn to ride the stirrups.

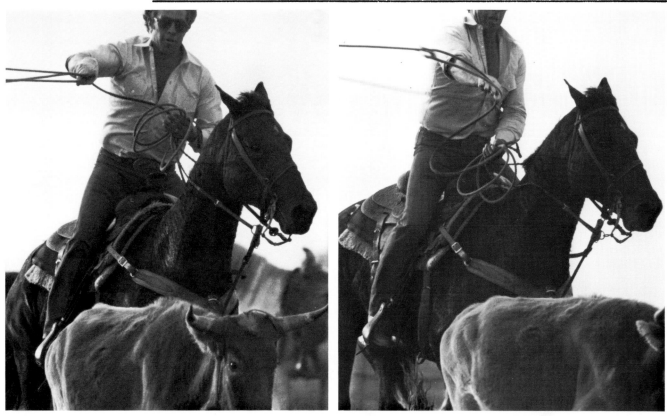

This is the ideal position for the header to be in when he wants to make a sure catch. The photo at right shows the loop as it is being released.

a stirrup length that works for you so you can lean forward a little and stand in the stirrups; don't sit flat in the saddle (refer to the section on horsemanship). You'll rope better and you'll help your horse run and move better by riding like this. I do this from the time we start a run until I've finished dallying.

As a header, you've got the entire length of the arena to work with. Your goal is to catch the steer as soon as you can, and then do whatever you can to put the steer in the best position for the heeler. The heeler wants the width of the arena to work in, so don't cheat him. Ideally, what the header wants to do is make his run in the shape of an "L." He chases the steer straight down the arena; he's coming in to the steer's left side, so if the steer is hazed a little toward the right side of the arena, that's even better — it will give the heeler that much more arena width to work with after the header has roped, dallied, and turned left at roughly a 90-degree angle (the other part of the L).

If a steer starts running to the left side of the arena, well, go ahead and make your catch and do the best you can. If the steer runs up next to the fence and you've got him roped, you'll

have to stop him along the fence, turn left, and angle out into the arena so the heeler has a chance to throw. You've got to get the steer away from the fence in order for the heeler to make his catch.

Remember when you throw the loop to follow through with arm and hand. Then grab the slack and pull it, rotating your thumb upwards! *Keep your thumb upwards throughout the dally.* If your thumb isn't up, it can get caught in the dally and be cut off, literally. Something else — *keep your eyes on the steer while you're dallying.* Never look down at the saddle horn; you can get into trouble if you're not watching the steer, ready to react to whatever he does. However, if you sense something is wrong at the saddle horn, undally immediately, kick the horse back into position, and then redally — *think.* When you start to dally the rope around the saddle horn, don't crimp it off tight in your hand. As I said earlier, there is rope running through my hands almost continually from the time I begin to swing the loop until I've finished with the dally. Let the rope continue to slip through your hand as you bring it around the saddle horn in a counter-clockwise motion.

Here's Reg heading. Look at the follow-through in his right arm. He is pointing exactly where he wants that loop to go.

Take one dally or two, or three or four if you want to and have enough tail left in your rope, then hold it tightly.

At this point, you should momentarily stop your horse straight. Don't try to turn your horse to the left before you dally, and don't turn him before the steer has hit the end of the rope. The horse can take the jerk of the steer on the end of that rope much better if he's straight to the steer rather than turned sideways when the jerk comes. A sideways jerk throws the horse off balance and hurts him. A horse takes a few bad jerks from the side and he learns to anticipate; he'll start dropping his shoulder, trying to get into the ground to get ready for that jerk, and that's when you'll hear ropers complain about having a horse that "ducks off." Sometimes you can take a horse like that, stop him straight a few times, and

Reg has pulled the slack, and raised his arm to dally.

35

Keep your eyes on the steer as you dally. If you sense something is wrong with your dally, undally immediately, continue to watch the steer, and kick the horse back into position.

Pull the slack down and back (above). Keep a relaxed grip on the rope as you dally (left); let a little rope slip through your hand if it wants to. Don't hold the rope absolutely tight until the dally is complete.

As you begin to dally, remember to have your wrist rotated so your thumb is at the top of your hand. Keep your thumb in this position throughout the dally.

this will help keep him honest — but the rider must be consistently honest with the horse if he expects the horse to be honest with him. And a horse that really gets into the habit of ducking off will never get over it.

The header should play with the momentum of the steer. If he's a fresh steer the header will have to "take hold" of him, stop him pretty good, and control him the best he can, because the steer will be wilder than a steer that's used to being roped. But even so, try to L that steer across the width of the arena. Your horse should be pulling the steer but not running off with him; naturally you don't want that steer to pull your horse, either.

If you know the steer has been roped a lot, you'll know that he may want to drag his heels or try to walk or trot instead of lope once you've headed him. In this case, you won't want to stop too hard; instead, keep as much mo-

mentum going as possible. Try to "round" the angle of the L to encourage the steer to keep moving the way he's supposed to. You want the heeler to see some action in those hind legs.

A lot of headers have a tendency to take hold of a steer and bring him straight back, almost in a 180-degree turn. That's bad for the heeler. A steer that is jerked back like that will start to play out or give up. And that makes it hard for the heeler to get into any kind of rhythm with the steer in order to make a catch. It also makes it hard for the heeler to get into position to make his throw. If the heeler is riding wide open, trying to get to the steer's left hip in time for the catch, and the steer suddenly does an about-face, that heeler will practically have to come to a sliding stop and do a roll-back in order to get into position again. So remember the L.

The header should be watching the

Take one dally or two, or as many as you want if you have enough tail left in the rope. On heavy cattle, the more dallies the better. Notice also how the coils and reins are held up and out of the way of the dally.

The rope is dallied and the horse is stopping straight with the steer. The horse won't come to a complete stop, but he'll be in a stopping position to absorb the initial jerk, then immediatley turn to the left.

The only way you'll know for sure what the steer is doing is to keep your eyes on him.

steer at all times after he has caught him. Oh, there will be occasions, say, if you know you're coming up close to the fence, or roping in a crowd, or you want to really get with your horse and urge him forward, when you'll glance ahead. Other than that, watch the steer — that's the only way you'll know for sure what he's doing, and what the heeler is doing.

After the heeler has made his catch, dallied, and stopped, he and the header have got to face one another with the steer in the middle. The header must anticipate everything coming tight, and turn around to the right, or "face up" accordingly. He doesn't want to hit the heeler hard, because the heeler can only hold the weight of the steer, not the weight of the steer and the heading horse. But he wants to make sure the ropes will be tight enough so the heeler

won't drop a foot out of the loop.

Some heading horses are trained to do a roll-back to the right when they face up, others turn off their front and let the hind legs move around. The style you use will be determined by the horse's ability; however, the roll-back can be hard on a horse because of the pressure of a heavy steer on the end of the rope.

The field flagger will drop his flag signalling for time as soon as both ropers are facing one another, with ropes dallied and taut with the steer in the middle. This is the end of the run. After the flag has dropped, both ropers should put some slack in their ropes; the steer will walk out of the heel loop, and the header can keep hold of his rope to help drive or guide the steer to the catchpen gate.

1/ Steer is released; header has started his horse in pursuit.

2/ Header "picks up" his rope, ready to swing.

3/ Moving toward the steer's left hip.

4/ Nearing position for the throw.

5/ Header is in position and horse begins to rate the steer.

6/ Horse continues to rate the steer as header swings.

7/ A perfect throw. The loop has encircled both horns and is starting to curl upwards. Header reaches for slack.

8/ Slack has been pulled and header has raised his arm to start the dally.

9/ The horse will begin to stop for a split-second, absorbing the jerk, then...

10/ ... begins to turn the steer at a 90-degree angle--the L.

11/ The steer has turned...

12/ ... and is being led across the arena.

13/ The header watches the steer and the heeler.

14/ The heeler has found his target.

15/ The heels are roped; the header continues to lead the steer...

16/ ... as the heeler pulls his slack.

17/ Heeler is ready to dally; header must anticipate when to stop pulling the steer and face up.

Be honest with
your horse, and
he'll be honest
with you.

1/ *Moving in for the catch. The horse is in the right lead.*

2/ *The action is starting to move to the left. The horse is
changing into the left lead.*

3/ *We're in position to head the steer.*

4/ *The horse should continue to run until the header asks him to stop.*

5/ *I'm completing my dally and am ready to ask the horse to stop.*

6/ *The horse is taking the first jerk; he started to turn a little earlier than I wanted him to, and I am holding him in position.*

Study the header's body position in this run.

1/ *Reg, roping on a horse still in training, displays perfect roping and riding form. He is riding the stirrups, not sitting flat in the saddle; his elbow is up and the loop is open.*

2/

3/ *His arm follows through with the throw (top), and he maintains complete control and balance, sitting back in the saddle slightly as he pulls his slack (bottom).*

4/

5/ *He's out of the saddle again as he begins to dally.*

6/

7/ *He begins to turn the steer into an L. The steer has not been jerked backwards into a 180-degree turn.*

8/

FROM THE GROUND

You should swing the loop at a little sharper angle than you would if you were throwing a head loop.

A sawhorse makes a good heeling dummy. Nearly everyone can find or build a sawhorse, and if you tie the front of that sawhorse to a fence, so the back legs are raised off the ground a few inches, you'll have a dummy you can actually catch—you'll be able to throw the heel loop and pull your slack.

Position yourself behind the dummy as you would if you were heading, behind the left hip. This is the position you'll want when you're heeling a steer. Build your loop, as we discussed in the previous section on heading; I like to use about the same length of spoke in the loop for heeling that I use for

heading. Swing the loop overhead and feed it, as discussed earlier, and look at your target, the legs.

You should swing the loop at a little sharper angle than you would if you were throwing a head loop. In other words, you want that loop to dip down in front of you and rise behind you as you're swinging. You're swinging the loop, feeding it to the size you want; your elbow twists upwards with each swing, rolling with the loop, keeping it open. Watch for the shot you want and adjust your loop at the same time, then make your throw and remember to follow through with your arm and hand, pointing where you

A simple sawhorse with the back legs lifted off the ground makes a good heeling dummy.

50

1/ *Feeding the loop--I've just released a coil.*

2/ *Elbow is up.*

3/ *I'm working on the angle I want the loop to follow.*

4/ *This is about as sharp as you want the downward angle of the loop. This angle will vary a little according to the distance you're standing (or riding) from the heels. From this angle, the target would be very close.*

5/ *Releasing the loop (left), and grabbing the slack.*

6/

want the loop to go.

The loop should be thrown with enough authority so it hits in front of the right hind leg and then curls around in front of both legs. The rope should have enough body to it so it actually stands on edge, resting against the back legs of the sawhorse. Look at the accompanying photos to see exactly how the loop should look after it has been thrown. At this point, if you were roping a steer, the steer's hind legs would be moving into the loop and you would hold your slack momentarily, then pull it as soon as the feet are in the loop.

For heeling, you want to grab the slack just like you would for heading — with the palm of your hand, thumb toward you, grasping the rope between thumb and forefinger and then curling the other fingers around the rope. But instead of pulling the slack straight down, as in heading, hold the slack and then pull it *upwards*. This upward pull on the rope will draw the

loop around the legs; the steer will also be pulling, taking even more slack out of the rope.

I should also mention that I usually pull my slack a little differently than many ropers. Rather than pull the slack straight up, in front of myself, I pull it upwards and then twist my arm and hand, so my thumb is down and the rope is pulling on the back side of my hand. In this manner, I can continue pulling slack behind myself to be extra certain that loop is drawn snugly around the legs. As the steer pulls my hand down, I rotate my hand so my thumb is up, and then I dally.

Whether you simply pull your slack straight up and dally, or pull the slack straight up and put this little twist in your arm and dally, it should be one fluid motion. And remember not to crimp the rope off tight in your hand; you'll be pulling on the rope, but the rope will also be slipping through your hand a little until you've completed the dally.

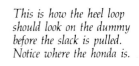

This is how the heel loop should look on the dummy before the slack is pulled. Notice where the honda is.

The loop looks the same heeling a steer, with the top part of the loop wrapping around the steer's legs just as his feet are ready to move forward.

1/ *Another view of the swing--my elbow is rotated upwards.*

2/ *I'm feeding the loop.*

3/ *Beginning to throw.*

4/ *The moment of release.*

5/ *Grabbing the slack.*

6/ *Pulling the slack.*

7/Quite often, I'll pull my slack and rotate my elbow so my thumb is down. By doing this I can extend my arm completely behind me, pulling more slack than I could by simply pulling the rope straight up. If I throw a smaller loop that hasn't been fed as much--at a steer that has been headed and turned exceptionally fast--I won't use this method because I won't have as much slack to pull.

8/ *My arm descends for the dally (top left and right), and my thumb has rotated up.*

9/

10/ *You can practice the motions of dallying.*

1/ *I'm swinging my loop, standing in the proper position for heeling.*

2/ *Elbow is up; honda is at the top of the loop.*

3/ *Elbow rotates and loop begins to roll.*

4/ *Loop is on my left side now and has rolled over--the honda is on the bottom.*

5/ *The loop is open and I'm making the throw (left). The loop arrives and I'm ready to pull the slack.*

6/

Roping heels "out of the air."

1/ *Another view.*

2/

3/

1/Watch the loop grow. I've got two coils in my hand at this point.

2/One coil begins to slip into the loop.

3/The loop continues to grow...

4/...and it is definitely larger at this point.

5/Ready to throw.

6/The throw...

7/... and the catch.
Same throw, same
results (below).

FROM THE HORSE

Walk him into that box, turn and stand somewhere off the back of it.

Tuck the loop under your arm and hold the saddle horn when you start.

I like to think of the heeler as the wide receiver of the team. The header, the quarterback, puts the play in motion, but it's up to the heeler to complete the play, and I feel his job starts the same time as the header's. The heeler rides along and has to watch the whole situation develop. As a heeler, you've got to watch the header and the steer so you can calculate when to be in position to complete the run. The header has a limited amount of time and room to work in, trying to set up an ideal situation for you to make a heel catch, but that ideal situation doesn't occur every time. You and your horse have got to be ready to react, to adjust to whatever does happen. If you've got a hard-running steer, you've got to suddenly be extra aggressive so

you won't be late when the header catches him and turns off. If you've got a slower steer, you've got to do what I call "idle" your horse up there, making sure you don't come in too quickly and interfere with the header's work.

The heel horse should be relaxed but alert, ready to adjust, ready to change leads if necessary, ready to give an extra burst of speed if he's asked for it. Walk him into that box, turn and stand somewhere off the back of it. Then tuck your loop under your right arm and hold onto the saddle horn with your right hand; or if you ride well enough to be able to move with the horse without holding onto the saddle horn, you can simply hold your loop out to the side if you prefer.

When the gate flies open and the

You can really get with your horse's motion by starting like this. You won't run the risk of getting off balance a little and hurting the start as you would if you weren't holding the saddle horn.

Sometimes the heeler has to hold his horse back just an instant so he doesn't interfere with the header.

Out of the box.

steer starts running with the header in pursuit, I don't care to have my heel horse involved in a horse race. The heel horse should burst out of the box, but he shouldn't be running wide open initially; if you've got a hard-running steer and you need to ask for more speed, then do it. But I see a lot of heelers who look like they're trying to race the header to the steer. They don't want to be late when the header turns the steer, which is good, but they aren't helping their partner by crowding up so close.

In a situation like that the header will have trouble swinging his loop without hitting the heeler. Or, if the header does make his catch, the heeler will find himself ahead of the action. He'll be between the header and the steer, and this will make the steer want to stop or drag his feet, putting more weight on the heading horse. The

heeler will have to stop or slow down in order to let the steer move ahead.

Look at the sequence of action photos in the next section, and you'll get an idea of how the heeler should move into position at the right time—not too soon and not too late. And remember, you should be riding your stirrups, not sitting flat in the saddle.

There is no set formula for getting into position because conditions vary. I can't say "ride six feet behind the header and then ride in three feet behind the steer for your catch"—be-cause there are too many variables. I do say you have to get a feel for how your header ropes and how his horse moves, and you have to ride your own horse well enough to react and adjust to what individual steers will do. Your goal is to be swinging your rope, and moving your horse into position behind

64

the steer's left hip just as the header turns him off to complete that L we talked about. The heeler, according to PRCA rules, can't throw until the steer has been turned by the header.

Swinging your loop brings up another point: Don't feel you have to start swinging as soon as you leave the box—unless you're roping over a short scoreline and your header makes a quick catch right out of the box. Over a longer scoreline, and with a fast steer, you'll wear out your arm if you swing the rope the length of the arena.

Learn to gauge when you need to start swinging as the run shapes up. What you're striving for is to be in a position to throw just as your loop has been fed to the size you want, and the shot becomes available.

Your horse should approach the steer's left hip and begin rating the steer at a distance that's actually a little closer than you want to throw your loop. Rating the steer like this gives you the opportunity to get into rhythm with the steer's movement. If your swing is out of rhythm initially, don't

Don't feel you have to start swinging the rope as soon as you leave the box.

Working for position (right). This is the rhythm you're looking for (below). The loop is forward, pointing toward the steer, as the steer's hind legs are extended back toward the rope. I'm in position for the throw.

slow it down to adjust, speed it up, then back off until you're in rhythm. And again, this timing and rhythm is just something you have to learn through practice.

As soon as you've got the rhythm—your loop is swinging in time with the steer's legs—let the steer progress on you a little so you can get the distance that you've been working for, the distance that's good for you to throw. There's an area in which you know you are confident in catching. When the steer progresses to that point, nail him. Make your throw as you stop your horse (but don't let the horse stop *before* you've thrown). The bottom of the loop should brush the ground and curl around the steer's legs just as it did on the roping dummy.

People ask about roping heels out of the air, like I do most of the time. Do I throw a different type of loop? Essentially, no. It's the same basic loop, the

same positioning and rhythm; my target is a little different. What the shot amounts to is this: I ride into the position I want, I'm feeding my loop, picking up the rhythm, then letting the steer move out on me a little, and I throw the loop so it hits the steer's feet when they're in the air, just starting to come down. I'm pulling up on the slack as the steer's feet are moving downward, then I dally.

With the regular heel catch, the loop arrives when the legs are in the ground and the steer is stretching for that next jump; and, of course, the steer jumps into the loop. I like to rope heels out of the air because I feel it's a little more precise loop, and it's quicker. But a steer has to be moving pretty good to make that kind of catch; by that I mean the steer should be in an up-and-down motion—his feet are in the ground and out of the ground. If a steer isn't showing much motion, dragging his feet badly, "shuffling" or trotting—not getting out of the ground—then I throw the regular heel loop.

The whole secret of heeling is to take

If you can get into position and pick up the rhythm, you'll make a catch.

things step by step; you don't want to get ahead of yourself. Ride in there, pick up the rhythm while the horse rates the steer, then let the steer get out there farther where you can make your catch. It's an anticipated shot, just like shooting clay pigeons; you lead the target, throwing ahead of the steer's hind legs. You want the loop to arrive just in time for the legs to move forward into it. Your horse should stop just as you throw, and as the steer moves into the loop, it's just a matter of pulling your slack and dallying. And you dally the same way heading or heeling, letting a little rope slip through your hands as you wrap the rope around the saddle horn once or twice and hold it. Don't let your horse run backwards, turn sideways, or go forward at this point. Just let him stand.

This all sounds like a lot of steps to go through, especially when you see the caliber of professional ropers in rodeo today, and look at times of less than five seconds. Do these ropers actually go through all of this deliberately, step-by-step, rating cattle and so forth? The obvious answer is no, not all the time. When the money is up and times are running fast, the pros combine this procedure into one fluid motion.

Perhaps, to win, there really isn't time for the heeler to do anything but dive into position as the header turns the steer, and then throw. If it works, it's sensational. But even though the catch may have been made when the heeler skipped a step, or was out of position, it was made as a result of the timing and rhythm learned through practice, step-by-step. And when the professionals practice, they devote a lot of time going through these steps at a slightly slower pace. You don't need to try to rope every practice steer in five seconds.

It's an anticipated shot, just like shooting clay pigeons.

1/ *The heel horse should stop and just stand.*

2/ *Keep your thumb up and don't crimp the rope tight in your hand...*

3/ *...until you've completed the dally. This is a one-wrap dally.*

1/*Don't crowd the header. Stay back just a little.*

2/*Watch and anticipate.*

3/*Reg has made the head catch, and I still haven't picked up my rope yet.*

Your goal is to be swinging your rope and moving your horse into position behind the steer's left hip just as the header turns him.

4/Reg is pulling his slack and I'm moving up closer, ready to get into position.

5/He's ready to dally and I'm starting to swing my rope.

6/I'm maintaining my position, waiting for the steer to be turned.

7/The head rope isn't completely tight yet, but the steer is already starting to fight.

8/We begin the turn and the steer is fighting the rope. He's a little wilder than some of the others, and will probably show me some good action with his heels, an ideal target.

He's a good steer to heel. He's in the ground and out of the ground; he doesn't drag or shuffle his feet.

9/*I'm ready to move into roping position as soon as the steer's hips have turned.*

10/*Now I'm working to get behind the steer's left hip.*

11/ *I'm getting closer and trying to pick up the rhythm.*

12/ *Because the steer is moving out well, the header doesn't want to get right in front of him or he might try to cut behind the header's horse.*

13/ *I'm in position and working to pick up the rhythm with the steer. I don't have it yet--my rope is over the steer's back, but his feet aren't extended.*

14/ *One more swing, a little faster, and...*

15/ *... I'm in time with the steer. My loop has just passed over the steer's back as his feet were extended.*

Swinging your loop in time with the steer's legs, picking up this rhythm, is something that comes from practice.

16/ Now for the throw.

17/ Two heels, out of the air.

A C T I O N

I've made comments on each sequence to point out specific things I think are important.

At this point, I think you'll find it helpful to look at a variety of team roping runs that were photographed from several angles. By studying these sequences, you'll get a better idea of how ropers and horses work together, and work with the steer's actions, to make a successful run.

This involves timing and the ability to react and adjust to whatever an individual steer does -- whether he runs fast or slow, goes straight or veers off; whether he shows good action in his hind legs or has a tendency to drag his heels. Look at the horses -- notice the leads and positioning. Look at the loops -- see how the slack and dallies are handled. I've made comments on each sequence to point out specific things I think are important.

— Leo

Note: Photographer Kurt Markus and I spent a memorable day at the Camarillo arena, acquiring these action photos. It was more fun than work, at least for us, and we were treated to one of the finest roping displays anyone will ever see. Kurt shot more than 1,200 exposures in the arena while Reg and Leo roped, and he learned after the first steer that his job would be fairly easy if he assumed the role of director -- Reg and Leo could rope a steer wherever he asked them to. Throughout the day, they roped around Kurt and his cameras; there must have been 100 runs altogether, and Reg never missed a head throw. Leo never missed a heel shot, but did allow one steer to slip one foot out of the loop -- he wasn't even trying to dally on that steer. Leo and Reg traded positions later that afternoon, and the roping continued.

Leo roped off his two top heeling horses, the veteran Stick and the younger gelding Shorty. Reg roped from two horses he was still training, and it occurred to me by the end of the day that the young heading horses probably had no idea what it was like for a rider to throw and miss.

Some of the steers had a tendency to veer away from Kurt as soon as they left the box, so Stick and Shorty would take turns as stationary hazers; whichever horse was resting would be placed by Leo just to the left of the roping chute, about 30 feet into the arena. The horse would stand patiently while the action passed by, with steers running true to form toward Kurt. At this point, the hard-running steers weren't about to turn from anything; their attention was directed toward the ropers, not Kurt. And it was that first steer in particular that gave Kurt a charge of adrenalin.

Kurt had asked Reg to just rope the steer and turn him in front of the camera -- he didn't say how close. Kurt was nearly ready to bolt for the fence as the steer bore down on him, but Reg's rope shot out at the last instant and settled around the horns; the steer was turned approximately four feet in front of the camera, and quickly heeled by Leo.

Kurt brushed dirt off his camera lens. "Maybe you should rope them just a little farther away," he suggested. Reg nodded; no problem.

We broke for lunch around noon,

and drove to a restaurant in town. Leo was driving, which was fine with Reg, who agreed that he had had enough driving when he was rodeoing for a living, roping with Leo.

"What are you talking about?" Leo chided. "I did the driving all those years." Leo went on with it, turning to others in the club-cab pickup: "The reason Reg quit rodeoin' is because it was his turn to drive."

Reg laughed at the joke, and the conversation turned to countryside observations. The roping resumed as soon as we returned to the arena.

It's always interesting to watch experts at work, no matter what task they are experts in performing. The two Camarillos at work that day were obviously experts in animal husbandry and training, as well as in roping. Horses and cattle were worked, but none were abused, not even slightly. By nightfall, the animals were hungry, not exhausted, and the Kingpin of the Camarillo Ranch -- old Stick -- decided to take care of himself.

Stick knew the roping was over, but now everyone was standing around visiting and joking. He watched Leo, and when Leo turned away, Stick took a couple steps toward the gate.

"Stick," Leo said, "where you goin'?" Stick froze in his tracks, but the tone in Leo's voice told the horse his master was not seriously ordering him to stand, as he had done periodically through the day when he was "hazing" steers.

Stick waited for the conversation to resume, then started to walk once again. He got outside the arena, halfway across a corner of the pasture enroute to the barn when Leo called to him again. Stick stopped momentarily. "Well," said Leo, "Stick says it's time to quit." The horse started walking again in the darkness; he nudged open a gate and walked behind the barn. There was a stack of choice alfalfa hay there, and Stick enjoyed it "free choice" for a minute while he waited for Leo to catch up and remove the saddle and bridle.
— *Randy Witte*

1/ *Here's a steer that likes to run with his head low, which makes it more difficult for the header to rope him. The solution is to not feed to a real large loop, then make sure you're in perfect position before you throw.*

2/ *This steer wasn't any problem for Reg.*

3/*Dally and stop.*

4/*Begin the turn.*

5/*Heeler moves toward the hip.*

6/*We're into the L.*

7/ *This steer doesn't want to be led, but he is showing action in his hind feet. I'm in position; Reg urges his horse on and keeps his eyes on me and the steer.*

8/*I'm in time with the steer.*

9/ *Here's the throw; I'll get these heels in the air.*

10/ *Pulling the slack while the header continues leading the steer.*

11/My arm starts moving down to dally.

12/The dally is complete, and Reg continues to move forward to make sure the ropes are tight enough to prevent the steer from getting a foot out of the heel loop. He'll turn and face up.

13/*Facing up.*

1/ *A hard-running steer.*

2/ *Reg stretches a little to make this head catch.*

3/ *The steer is headed. We're going for fast time.*

4/ *I'm as close to the steer as I can be without bumping him or running past.*

87

5/ *The steer turns and his back end whips away from me.*

6/ *I'm not in an ideal heeling position but I can make this work.*

7/ *The steer was heeled one jump after he turned.*

8/ *We did it!*

1/ *Here's the type of run you should strive for.*

2/ *Header moves up quickly; heeler stays far enough away so he doesn't interfere with header.*

3/ *Ideal position for the head catch.*

4/Header pulls slack as heeler moves in closer and begins to swing.

5/Header dallies and heeler maintains his position.

6/Into the turn.

7/A heavy steer--he turns a little slower and the heeler reins to the right a bit so he doesn't get ahead of the action.

8/Heeler is "there on time."

9/Rating the steer, picking up the rhythm between loop and legs.

10/ *Steer wants to shuffle his feet; header pulls a little faster to increase the action.*

11/ *One more swing and I'll be in rhythm.*

12/ *The catch.*

13/ *The pull.*

14/ *The dally.*

15/ *This team roping is fun.*

1/ *Here's a good example of a header working to help a steer pick up momentum.*

2/ *The steer is headed and he just wants to stop.*

3/ *The header turns into the L and senses that this steer might "give up" and drag his heels if he is completely overpowered by the heading horse.*

4/Header continues to lead the steer--at a moderate pace.

5/The steer is moving, and the heeler can see a little action in the back legs.

6/ *Header keeps his eyes on steer and heeler.*

7/ *The steer is shuffling his feet now--not a good target. The header will lead him a little faster, trying to get better action in those heels.*

98

8/ *Riding the stirrups, watching the heels. The steer is moving better with this stride, but the heel loop will still have to be thrown low to the ground.*

9/ *This swing will deliver.*

10/ *The throw.*

1/ *This steer wants to veer in front of the heeler. The action is moving to our right, and both horses are in the right lead.*

2/ *The steer carries his head a little low--a more difficult target for the header.*

3/Reg got him! He's pulling slack and I've picked up my rope.

4/ *Now for the dally.*

5/ *The heading horse begins to turn and picks up the left lead.*

6/ *My heel horse is now in the left lead.*

7/ *This steer has a lot of action--he'll be fun to heel.*

8/*I'm still feeding my loop and moving into position.*

9/*Picking up the rhythm.*

10/ *The heel shot is becoming available.*

11/ *I let the steer progress on me and make my throw. My horse has nearly stopped as I begin to pull the slack.*

12/ *The heel horse just stands as I pull slack...*

13/ *... and dally.*

1/Starting the L.

2/The steer is taking his first jump into the turn and I'm making my throw for the heels.

3/The fast times come when the heeler can catch on that first jump into the turn. It's important for your horse to respond to a fast throw, and be ready to stop as soon as you signal him to, or he may put a front foot in the loop.

1/ *This shows good position between the header and heeler. The heeler shouldn't crowd the header while he's trying to make a head catch.*

2/ *When the header has made his catch the heeler can pick up his rope and get ready to move closer to the steer.*

3/ *This steer definitely doesn't want to be led.*

4/ *A header can take his eyes off the action for a moment when he really wants to get with his horse and urge him into a stronger pull. When a horse needs help in a situation like this, the rider can give it to him by riding in a balanced position, not looking back.*

111

5/ *Heeled. Now to pull slack.*

6/ *Starting the dally.*

7/My horse Stick knows his job is done on this run.

H O R S E S

Horsemanship

Good horsemanship is an important, but often overlooked, factor for success in team roping or any other timed event in rodeo. I grew up riding horses as well as roping, so this came naturally to me. But a lot of contestants in rodeo today didn't have that opportunity. A person may be a good roper on the ground, but if he lacks ability in horsemanship he won't rope effectively on a horse.

If you're not comfortable in the saddle, if you have trouble controlling a horse, then you need to do a lot of riding. Read books and articles on horsemanship, go to a horsemanship school if you have the means, watch how good horsemen handle their horses and ask them questions—all of this will help. But I really think the most important thing is to just do a lot of riding. Get out of the arena; ride in open country if possible. Get to know your horse and learn how to keep your balance.

Find a stirrup length that is short enough for you to stand in the saddle, but not so short that when you stand you lose your balance. By riding the stirrups and keeping your balance, you'll keep your weight closer to the horse's withers, off his back, and he'll be able to move more freely. Naturally, you don't stand in your stirrups all the time, but you do while your horse is actually working, or when you are trotting or loping him, warming him up.

When you do sit in the saddle, sit on your crotch, not on your tailbone. The stirrups should be squarely under your body, feet parallel to the ground.

Make sure you and your horse know your leads—a horse will usually take up the proper lead, left or right, on his own when he's loping or running without a rider, but he may not pick up the proper lead automatically with a rider because he can't always anticipate what the rider wants to do. If a rider sud-

denly reins in another direction it can take the horse by surprise, especially if the rider is off balance or doesn't help the horse by cueing him. The cue is to rein the horse in the direction you want to go, and at the same time lean slightly forward into that direction and bump the horse with your outside foot. If you were going left, the outside foot would be your right foot.

I want my horse to pick up the proper lead when we change directions as soon as I lean whichever way we should go. It's a natural movement, one the horse should pick up immediately, without any exaggerated cueing—this comes from practice and training, being as one with your horse.

When a horse is moving to the left, and he is in the left lead, his right front foot will hit the ground first, followed by the left foot, which hits farther ahead of the right and "leads" it. The same thing happens with the hind legs; the right hind leg will hit first, followed by the left, which hits farther ahead. When a horse is working to the right, and is in the right lead, the left feet hit first, followed by the right feet, which hit farther ahead.

Most team roping horses seem to start a run in the right lead, but it really doesn't matter which lead a horse picks up initially, as long as the horse can adjust to the situation. If a steer is running at an angle, right or left, the horse will have to pick up the proper lead or the steer will outrun him. The heading horse will have to take the left lead to complete that L we talked about, and the heel horse will have to take the left lead at that time in order to get into position.

You can work on leads while you're loping in a circle; lope in one direction for a little while, then turn to the outside of the circle and go the other direction. By turning to the outside, you're giving the horse the opportunity to change leads naturally. Work like this should be done at a collected lope; you should ride the stirrups and maintain control, if necessary, with a light "check" on the reins, "bumping" the horse's mouth by lightly pulling and releasing the reins in a rhythmic manner until the horse has settled into whatever gait you desire.

Often a beginner gets on a good rodeo timed-event horse and finds that the horse wants to run away with him; he's squeezed his legs around the horse, trying to stay in the saddle, and hauled back on the reins, thinking this will make the horse slow down or stop. But these actions just tell the horse to run, especially if he's a horse who spent time at a race track and was trained to run into the bit.

1/Action is moving to our left—both horses are in the left lead.

2/You can't make a turn like this if the horse is in the wrong lead.

3/I'm riding the stirrups, maintaining light control with the rein. The horses are still in the left lead, although the heading horse was jerked off balance for an instant and had to pick up the right lead with his front feet for one stride to regain his balance.

115

TRAINING

I think it's important for my horses to know when they've done well, and to know that I'm pleased with them, that I'm glad they're part of my team.

The key to training an inexperienced horse — one that is well broke and not afraid of a rope but doesn't know anything about team roping — is to actually be able to rope a steer off him. This is why a person has to ride and rope well enough, at the same time, in order to teach the horse. If a person can concentrate on maneuvering his horse into the correct position, and then catch the steer every time, the horse will learn what he is supposed to do. This is why a beginner shouldn't try to train his own horse. The horse won't know what to do to help the roper, and the roper won't be able to catch effectively in order to show the horse what is expected of him.

One thing I absolutely demand of a heel horse is that he not go past that imaginary line where the steer is turned back. A heel horse should be taught that no matter what, he must not run past that steer. If that ever happens during a practice or training session, I discipline the horse immediately; perhaps I'll whack him along the shoulder once with the tail of my rope (but you don't want to overdo this, or the horse may develop a fear of ropes). Incidentally, I think it is unprofessional for anyone to discipline his horse in competition. Do your schooling at the practice arena.

By the same token, when a horse does something I really like during a training session, I'll stop immediately and reward him. I'll do this by dismounting and loosening the cinches. I'll give him a kind word and a pat. A horse can understand that, and after all, that's the only reward he gets out of the game. I think it's important for my horses to know when they've done well, and to know that I'm pleased with them, that I'm glad they're part of my team.

I'll also use the reward technique for a young horse that is having a problem with a particular "pressure point," as I call it. Say I'm working with a horse who is exceptionally nervous in the box. Well, I'll spend time backing him in the box, and then getting off and loosening the cinches, letting him stand and relax. He'll learn that the box isn't a bad place to be. I'll spend time sitting on him in the box, like we're ready to rope, but when the steer is released, I'll hold him back; we won't rope. We may rope a steer and then stay in the box while two in a row go out; and then rope a few in a row and sit there while another gets turned out. This is called "scoring." The horse learns to be ready to run out of that box, but not until I ask him to.

A young horse in training also needs to learn to rate cattle, as I mentioned earlier in the book. If he's not a ranch horse, used to being around cattle, he'll need time just to get acquainted with them. Spend time swinging your loop and just following a steer down the arena, holding the horse in the position you want him to maintain, behind the steer's left hip. Don't let him run past the steer, and when he does a good job, stop and reward him.

It doesn't hurt any horse to learn how to "log," but it's essential for the heading horse to learn this. Logging is the term used to describe pulling — it's what the heading horse does once the steer has been roped; the heading horse pulls the steer across the arena. You train a horse to do this by tying a rope onto a log or some other weighted object, dallying, and having the horse pull the object around the arena. Start with a light object — the horse may spook at first when he finds he is dallied onto something, so stay at a walk and don't let the horse get out of control. And let the rope go if you do get into trouble. Be calm and patient — he'll gradually accept this pulling, and then you can graduate up to heavier objects, and of course steers.

You can teach the horse to face up while you're logging. Take the inside rein (the right side) and pull it around while you bump the horse's hind end around with your right foot. If you're working on a roll-back to face up, it helps the horse if you loosen the dally a little as you ask him to roll back over his hocks. Again, whichever method you use will depend on the horse, and one method of facing up isn't necessarily

Teach your horse to stand quietly when he is saddled and bridled and you have to leave him untied for a little while.

better than the other.

One more training hint — teach your horse to stand tied; teach him, with the use of hobbles, to stand still even if he isn't tied, when he is saddled and bridled and you have to walk away from him for awhile. This habit pays off when the horse is around a busy arena; there's nothing more irritating than to have to hunt up your horse after you've left him for a few minutes.

CARE & CONDITIONING

If a person really thought about all the factors involved with team roping, he'd say, "This can't work. There are too many variables." The point is, there are five things that have to come together properly for a successful run — two ropers, two horses, one steer — five chances for something to go wrong.

You don't have much control over what the steer is going to do, at least not until you rope him. But you gain greater control over the situation when you and your horse work together as one. If you can ride and rope, and you and your horse are working as a single unit, then it has got to work. The only other advantage available is to acquire an understanding of cattle, and we'll touch on that later. Right now, let's discuss the horse, an important part of your team.

A team roping horse has got to be in good physical condition if you plan to do a lot of roping on him. Care and conditioning become even more important if the horse is forced to undergo the stress of hauling to a lot of rodeos. Hauling is harder on a horse than the actual arena work. This is one reason why I like to give my horses a vacation periodically, let one rest while I haul another. Here's what I do to get a horse back in shape after he has been turned out for awhile to rest and relax,

117

and has become a little fat and soft in the process.

I like to have at least six weeks to two months, maybe even three months if there is time, to slowly condition a horse, physically and mentally, to get him ready for a lot of roping and hauling. I start by cutting way down on his hay, and increasing his protein. I'll usually start giving him whole oats once a day, and a little alfalfa hay twice a day, and then gradually increase the oats to a twice-a-day feeding, along with a little hay each time; of course he won't have regular access to any pasture. At the same time, I'll give him a one- to two-hour workout daily. I'll do a lot of walking at first, a little trotting and loping; the secret is to be long and light in those workouts initially.

As time goes by, I increase the protein and increase the work. The horse is losing weight, but he's getting the energy to do more work, and his muscles are getting toned. I'll keep him on this type of diet while we're rodeoing, until it's time to give him another break, at which point he'll go back to more roughage and less protein.

I like to feed twice a day, every 10 to 12 hours if I can. Naturally, when we're on the road, this feeding schedule can go to pieces; instead of feeding at 7 a.m. and between 5 and 7 p.m., I'll sometimes be forced to feed at 7 a.m. and midnight, or noon and midnight. I don't want to feed a horse just before I ask him to work; I figure I can compete better on an empty stomach, and so can the horse. If I'm scheduled to rope around feeding time, morning or

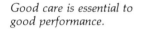

Good care is essential to good performance.

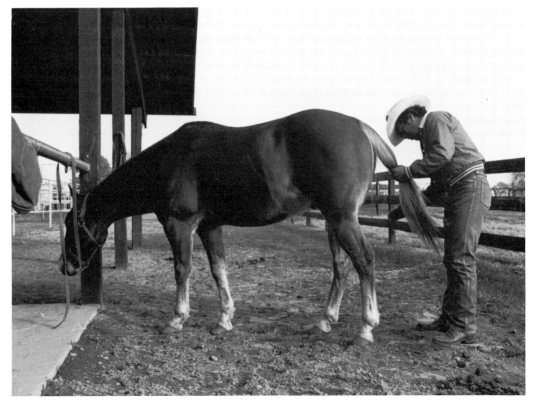

night, I might give the horse a little grain just to keep his mind off of eating, but wait until we're through working to give him a full feeding.

I want the horse to have a chance to excel. Part of that chance comes with a good long warm-up period before we rope. I'll start by walking, and then I'll do some loping in circles. I'll be standing in the stirrups while I keep him in a relaxed, collected lope. If we're going to the left, I want the horse to be in the left lead; if we're going to the right, he should be in the right lead. The horse should be responsive and respectful, collected and cooperative. He should be warming up his mind as well as his muscles. That's what this warm-up period is all about.

Before we're through warming up, I

A collected lope...

...in a circle.

Warming up the horse's mind as well as his body.

like to find a place in the arena, or perhaps on the track next to the arena, to let him run, really open him up for 50 or 100 yards, let him blow. I'll do this once or twice. This is especially important at a rodeo like Salinas, Calif., or Cheyenne, Wyo., where you're roping over extra-long score-lines, and your horse is going to have to do some real running before you even get close to whatever you're trying to rope.

When I pull into a roping, I like to have at least an hour to warm up. Again, sometimes the schedule doesn't allow this much time. There are occasions when a roper arrives late, has to unload and get ready to rope in a hurry. When this happens, you just try to condense the warm-up; you try to get as much as you can from it. I will say, under conditions like this, when a horse hasn't been properly warmed up, that a person is risking injury to his horse as well as the possibility of a poor performance.

I don't have the cinches pulled real tight during the warm-up, but I do pull them up tight just before I rope. Some people think they're doing their horses a favor by not cinching them tight, but I disagree. I believe the horse is more comfortable while we compete, and there is less risk of injury, if that saddle is snug enough to stay in place, rather than slipping a little when we tie onto

a steer. But don't forget to loosen the cinches when you're through with the run. When I'm practicing, I may run three or four steers back-to-back with-out loosening the cinches, but when I give the horse a breather, I'll loosen the cinches immediately. This is just com-mon sense and part of taking care of a horse, but I see a lot of people who forget about it.

Something else to be aware of is where you tie your horse. At any rodeo or roping, there are lots of horses, and it seems like everyone has to leave his horse tied periodically to pay an entry fee, or check the draw, or get a soft drink...whatever. Don't tie your horse to something that will in-jure him if he gets spooked, and try not to tie your horse too close to other horses. A person may absent-mindedly tie his horse next to a cranky mare or even a stud, and first thing you know his horse gets kicked. Things like that happen when you don't pay attention. I always try to tie my horse by himself; of course, someone else may come along the next minute and tie there too, so I have to keep an eye out for poten-tial trouble.

I mentioned that hauling is hard on a horse. Some people like to put leg wraps on their horses in an effort to help support the legs and maybe pre-vent injury inside the trailer. I don't use wraps; I think my horses are more

Tighten the cinches just before a run, then loosen the cinches right after a run.

You can lead a horse to water, but you can't make him drink--unless he's a rodeo horse who figures out he better drink whenever he has the chance.

comfortable without them. But if a person thinks his horse does better with leg wraps, fine, as long as he knows how to apply them properly so they're not too tight or too loose.

One thing I do to lessen the stress on my horses' legs while they're in the trailer is to have three to five inches of sawdust spread on top of the floor mats. This has a cushioning effect, provides good footing, and seems to encourage a horse to urinate in the trailer. Some horses don't want to urinate until they're unloaded, and this can lead to kidney problems.

I do try to take time, every few hours if possible, to find a safe place along the road to stop and unload the horses, giving them a chance to stretch and relax, and perhaps to drink. I've never had much problem with horses that didn't drink water when they had the chance, but some people do have horses like that. Sometimes a horse, especially a young one not accustomed to travel, will absolutely refuse water. Well, you've just got to stop, finally, and give the horse enough time to relax and get his bearings, and then he'll drink. If a horse is hauled regularly, though, it usually doesn't take him long to figure out that he better drink water whenever he has the chance.

And that brings up another point: be careful where you water your horse. I usually avoid community water tanks, and thus avoid the risk of having my horse pick up a disease. I have my own water buckets, and it's easy to lead a horse to a water tap, fill a bucket, and let him drink from that.

I also think it's a good idea, while traveling down the road, to have a first-aid kit along for your horse. It doesn't have to be elaborate, but should at least contain some kind of antiseptic to put on minor scrapes or cuts, some butazolidin for leg soreness, colic, or minor muscle injuries, and it might be wise to carry along a dose of tranquilizer. I've heard of horses involved in trailer accidents who survived the initial wreck, but went on to hurt themselves badly when they found themselves trapped and struggled to get free. In a case like this, it might save a horse if you could tranquilize him while you were waiting for help to get him out of an overturned trailer.

Rounding out your horse care program includes having him wormed and vaccinated regularly, and having him properly shod. You should also have his teeth checked periodically. And I would also like to encourage rodeo and roping committees to make sure they work up their arenas adequately. We can cope with weather conditions, but it's tough on a horse to work on hard or real cloddy ground. Some committees take excellent care of their arenas; I just wish they all did.

PRACTICING

Training and practice sessions are important to me. I like to have plenty of time; I don't want to hurry anything. I want to show the horse what's expected of him, and have him work willingly, not out of fear or pain. I don't like severe bits or other gimmicks that may get a horse's attention for awhile, but will prove useless in the long run. I seldom wear spurs; I think most horses, properly trained, will perform better without spurs. I ask a horse to give 100 percent effort in competition only; I don't expect a horse to give his utmost every time I run a practice steer.

A horse can give maximum effort much of the time, if he is allowed to rest physically and mentally. Asking a horse to continually give everything he has, run after run, or asking for more than he is capable of giving, will burn him out. He'll blow up and quit working altogether.

Spend a lot of time in the box without roping --show the horse that the box isn't a bad place to be.

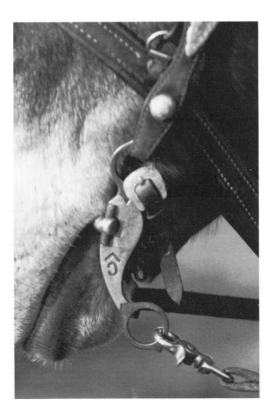

Different horses respond to different bits. Stick really doesn't need much of a bit, because of his disposition and willingness to work, so I use this light broken-snaffle on him.

122

I believe that man and horse will both have good days and bad. I don't dwell on the bad days, but try to analyze mistakes. If I miss, I ask myself: "Was it my fault or the horse's fault? Was it a combination of these or was it a result of the conditions or circumstances?" If I decide I made the mistake, I'll think about it and correct it. If the horse made a mistake, I'll work to correct the horse next time I practice.

Inside view of the Camarillo barn.

Barn and corrals at the Camarillo Ranch.

CATTLE

Top-quality Corrientes-- Mexican steers-- are ideal for roping.

When I practice, I like to be considerate of the cattle; for that matter, I want to take care not to injure a steer at a rodeo. Team roping is a humane event, but you've still got to use good judgment. If you're running a steer wide open and coming to the end of the arena, pull up to make sure the steer doesn't run blindly into the fence. Once the steer has turned, you can still go ahead and rope if you want to.

During practice, I may run a set of steers five or six times, but I won't tire them out much because of the way I practice. If I'm heeling, a lot of times I won't even dally; I'll make my catch and just hold the rope, and if the steer pulls it out of my hand, I'll get off my horse and pick it up. Or even if the heeler is dallying, he and the header can make sure the ropes don't come together so tight that the steer is pulled down. When heading during a practice session, I usually choose to take a steer to the catchpen after a run, rather than take the head rope off in the arena. This is especially important for fresh steers—you don't want them to get in the habit of stopping after they've been roped. And I always use horn wraps to prevent rope burns around the steers' horns.

I can do a lot of roping like this, and won't injure or tire the steers. Tired cattle develop bad habits—they may start ducking off to the side of the arena, rather than running straight; or they may run with their heads lowered, making it difficult for the header to rope; or drag their heels after they've been headed, making it difficult for the heeler to catch.

Slowly moving steers down an alleyway next to the arena. Let 'em take a little time.

Top quality Corrientes — Mexican steers — are ideal for roping. They're honest and hearty. Unfortunately, they are also expensive — you pay a premium for the horns, and when the cattle have grown too big to rope, it's hard to get your money back when they're sold as stocker or feeder cattle, even though they've gained weight. If you don't have access to Corrientes, then rope whatever breed of cattle you can; you can rope "muleys" (cattle without horns), and there are even artificial horns available that can be strapped around a muley's head. Domestic cattle tire more easily than Corrientes, but they're sure better than having no cattle at all to rope.

PROFILE

THE LION AT LARGE

Don't say he's gifted. As well as Leo Camarillo ropes, as easy as he makes it look, do not be misled into thinking he acquired his talent easily. In a sense, though, he did learn to rope naturally, because he started roping at a very early age. Leo is among the fifth generation of Camarillos who have lived in or around California's Orange County, and through the years roping has been important to the men in the family who worked as ranch and rodeo cowboys.

It all started with Leo's great-great-grandfather, Cavianno Camarillo, who rode from Sonora, Mexico to California around the turn of the century to work the ranges around Santa Ana. Cavianno was a good man with a reata.

Each succeeding generation learned to rope, but it was Leo's father, Ralph, who really became a fanatic about it. Ralph won the California calf roping championship in 1947, and still ropes for pleasure. No Little League father could have pushed his sons harder to learn a sport at a more impressionable age.

When Leo and his younger brother Jerold were barely beyond the toddler stage, Ralph fixed the boys up with miniature ropes so they could practice roping pop bottles in the living room. That story has been repeated often through the years, and it conjures up a happy vision of small boys playing with small ropes. The reality of those days, however, makes them seem not so happy. There were times when Leo and Jerold didn't care to spend a portion of the evening roping bottles, but there was never any alternative — daily roping practice was mandatory.

"Sometimes I hated to pick up a rope," Leo recalls.

"I cried a lot of the time," says Pilar Camarillo, their mother.

Pilar's family also goes back five generations in Orange County. Her great-grandfather was from France; he married an Indian woman and settled near San Luis Rey, where he bought a ranch that stayed in the family until the mid-1960s. But while Pilar's people were ranchers, they never attached any special significance to roping, and that was partly why she was upset with Ralph. She thought he was pushing the boys too hard. Ralph told her Leo and Jerold would love roping when they were older.

Practice sessions moved outdoors as the boys grew and started roping regular dummies. They also spent time each day learning to ride. Ponies that were trained to head or heel steers were their first mounts. Leo would do the heading; he was a year older than Jerold, and could throw a loop farther. The boys roped with each other, and with their father. They outgrew the ponies and started riding regular ranch horses. They learned to rope cattle in the open, and heeled calves at brandings.

"Our dad never tried to give us a lot of technical advice on roping," says Leo. "He showed us the fundamentals and told us to practice until we could catch something. If we were heeling calves at a branding, we were expected to catch two feet every time. If we missed, he made us get off our horses and go to work with the ground crew, where you had to do some *real* labor. He figured that would make us appreciate roping next time, and it did. We were afraid to miss."

This wasn't as bad a case of child abuse as it sounds. "We never really felt abused," Leo said. "He pushed us hard, but he always seemed to know when to back off, just before we blew up."

There was other pressure, though. For Leo, there was the responsibility of

126

Reg expounds on the qualities of his fine cowdog.

protecting his younger brother at school. Whether this entailed crossing a busy street safely, or engaging in fisti-cuffs with bullies, Leo felt responsible for Jerold's welfare. There was also racial prejudice—Leo was the darkest youngster in class, and the child who is different always suffers. Leo hated school and dreamed of someday wreak-ing vengeance on those he considered enemies.

Roping became important to both Leo and Jerold when they were teen-agers. For one thing, they were good at it; they could beat a lot of men they roped against at local jackpots. The ropes became great equalizers in a world of inequality. Ralph gradually quit driving his boys to excel because they were driving themselves. Any frustration or anger pent up from school was channeled into competition.

There were never enough cattle to rope. No one ropes ranch cattle unless there is a need for it, such as doctoring or branding. So every Sunday Ralph and his sons would load up horses and drive to one of the area roping arenas

where they practiced and competed at the same time. For Leo and Jerold, the uppermost thought was that if they won money, they would be able to buy lunch at the school cafeteria that week, rather than packing a lunch from home. The prestige and money that goes with winning were important to them, and they continued to wear out dummies during the week.

Leo became a rodeo fan as well as contestant. He attended every big rop-ing or rodeo he could to watch and learn, and especially enjoyed hanging around the venerable California stock contractor, Andy Jauregui. Leo knew the broncs and bulls in several rodeo strings as well as the riders did. But he paid extra close attention when the top professional ropers competed. He would watch their various styles of roping, and when he saw something that seemed especially effective, he would return home and try to duplicate the feat on the dummy.

He and Jerold spent so much time working out on dummies that it was inevitable for them to practice trick throws, just to break the monotony. They did everything but stand on their heads, throwing loops from awkward positions. They were intrigued with throwing a heel loop that was so precise it didn't touch the ground.

"We started roping heels out of the air just for fun, and did it for several years before we really knew what we were doing, or knew what we had going for us," Leo remembers. That style was foreign to most ropers in those days. "It wasn't a style we learned from anyone; it just seemed natural to heel that way. I know I took a little bit of everyone else's style and gradually came up with my own."

Leo and Jerold's cousin, Reg Camarillo, grew up in Los Angeles but spent summers at the ranch. Leo and Jerold roped, so Reg roped. By the time all three had finished high school, they were comrades in arms, determined to make a living in rodeo, and ready to "out-gun" the older generation of team ropers.

They rented a room downtown at the Oakdale Hotel for a dollar a day, and lived on ice tea and hamburgers. They gleaned cash from local jackpots during the week with devastating regularity, and worked every amateur rodeo they could get to on weekends. Leo was primarily a header in those days, but wasn't satisfied with his winnings no matter who his partner might be. He was a good header, but there were lots of good headers then. There weren't as many good heelers, it seemed, so he decided to devote his ef-

They rented a room downtown at the Oakdale Hotel for a dollar a day, and lived on ice tea and hamburgers.

A team that made rodeo history.

A man of determination and dedication.

forts to heeling. For Leo, it made all the difference.

A lot of the bread-and-butter jackpots, casually run affairs, started banning the Camarillos from competition — the three young men were winning too much money; it was like turning the lions in with the Christians. And Leo wasn't exactly a graceful winner in those days. The Lion took pleasure in telling other ropers that he intended to win their money — and then he did win it. Sometimes he would pull into a roping and, just for devilment, engage Jerold in a rehearsed conversation, within earshot of all, that went something like this:

"I'll bet you a thousand dollars I can rope every steer today in less than nine seconds," Leo would brag, knowing even a ten-second run was out of reach for most of the ropers there.

"Well, I'll bet $1,500 I can rope all mine in less than eight," Jerold would respond.

The Camarillos might go ahead and rope the way they had bet that day, but Leo laughs about it now, and is truthful about the wagers. "We'd bet all this money among ourselves and make it sound serious, but many times we wouldn't have even a dollar's worth of change in our pockets. The talk sure unnerved the competition, though."

The local ropers weren't too sad in 1968 when the Camarillos departed their ranks and stepped up to the Rodeo Cowboys Association. It was Leo and Jerold at first — Reg had been drafted into the Army during the Viet Nam war. The brothers roped with several heading partners, and nothing changed except that they won more money on the professional level. Leo won more money than any other rookie that year, but was given the dubious distinction of becoming the first such winner not to receive the Rookie of the Year Award. His habit of inflicting brash remarks on others rankled the association's board of directors, who retaliated by giving the award to the next man in line. Such a decision will probably never be repeated, considering the possible legal ramifications, not to mention the moral ones. But Leo was so incensed at the snub that he went to his first National Finals determined to win the average. And that's what he and header Billy Wilson did.

There have been many trophy saddles and buckles since then for Leo. Most of the saddles — more than 60 of them won at rodeos across the country — are piled up in tack rooms, one atop another, collecting dust. A dozen or so of the most expensive gold, silver, and jeweled trophy buckles are stored in a safe deposit box at the bank near the old Oakdale Hotel.

Jerold and Reg both live on small ranches just outside of Oakdale, but Leo lives an hour's drive away near the town of Lockeford. There he and his wife Sharon live on the perfect rodeo ranch. They've bought and sold land before, but finally settled on a piece of property with irrigated pasture along a quiet road, five minutes driving time from the freeway and 45 minutes from the Sacramento airport.

Sharon's brother, an architect, helped design the house, and the result is an impressive and comfortable home, complete with sunken living room and rock fireplace. A separate trophy room adjoins the house.

Their stable is well built and efficient, with individual box stalls and pipe-fenced runs. A workroom and storage area are on one end, and beyond that is Leo's office. A secretary is there each day to answer the phone, take messages, and also handle the routine chores when Leo and Sharon are on the road.

Out back is the arena, where the couple practice and work with horses. Leo has roped as many as 100 steers in a single day.

"I've always said I rope because of the money, but really, I think I rope for the love of it," he says. "Roping is on my mind constantly, every day; I'm either practicing, competing, or thinking about it. I'm always trying to improve. And I also know I'm in a profession that demands this type of work and dedication in order to remain successful. A man who rodeos for a living

has got to have it on his mind constantly or he'll starve to death in short order."

Leo believes aspiring ropers should set their goals and draw a line: "Do you want to rope for fun, or do you want to rope for a living? There is a difference, and sometimes the difference is happiness or misery, satisfaction or frustration.

"Rodeo schools or clinics are good for this reason alone," he continues. "They help a student realize what it takes to make a living or win a championship at roping, and what it takes to rope well enough just to have an enjoyable hobby. But whatever a person's goal is, he shouldn't be afraid to compete with the pros."

Leo disdains the concept of "non-winner" ropings — contests that are closed to those who have won a certain amount of money. It isn't the easy

"I think I rope for the love of it."

"Don't be afraid to rope with the pros."

prize money he is after — the cash usually doesn't amount to much. "The point is," he says, "no one improves his roping through a lack of competition. I don't care if you're roping for 25 cents or $2,500, competition is what contest team roping is all about. Competition makes all the hard work of practicing worthwhile. It brings out the best in people."

Leo thrives on competition. "The highlight of the whole year for me is to go to the National Finals Rodeo. That's what rodeoing for a living means. I've got to be in the Finals — every year — and experience all the pressure that goes with that last steer. When I can feel that pressure, and then overcome it and win, then I am satisfied. That's the climax."

Pressure is all in the mind, he believes, and if it is channeled properly, it can be used to advantage — the adrenalin starts flowing. "When you get right down to it, there isn't much difference in a practice run and a run for the money. You just know you have to do what you are capable of doing. A

person gains confidence from all those hours of practice. There have been times when I've spent days practicing and thought to myself, 'As much time as I'm spending in this arena, there must be someone out there I can beat.' It's almost like an act of God, like He's telling me, 'If you work as hard as you possibly can, I'll see that you are rewarded.'"

There are limits to the work, even for Leo. He has physically collapsed a couple of times — friends took him to the hospital. The culmination of too many long drives, too many hours of practice, and too many rodeos in too little time caught up with him. During one of his hospital stays, he slept for 48 hours. "I'd brought it on myself. I wasn't getting enough rest, wasn't eating properly, wasn't drinking enough water. Both times, after I was forced to rest, and then got back on a good diet with lots of protein, I just sort of cured myself."

He has learned to pace himself better in recent years. His rest periods are important to him, and he may rest for a

Adorning one wall of his tack room are Leo's favorite posters: Farrah and Snoopy.

day or two, or perhaps a week, after a particularly grueling rodeo run. He views his rest as a reward, if he has won. If he hasn't won, he'll still take the rest, out of necessity, "but it won't be rewarding to me. I'll be extra anxious to get back on the road again."

The road is his home. "I like the road; I like the travel involved with rodeo. I'm proud of my house and property, and I like to be there with Sharon. But until I retire from rodeo, the road will be my real home."

Leo is like an alarm clock. He winds himself up gradually while he sits in his office, handling arrangements for an upcoming tour of rodeos that might see him driving and flying across the country for a week, two weeks, or more than a month without a rest. But he is careful not to release the adrenalin too quickly. "It's something that starts building inside me. If I've got several days before I leave on a trip, I won't think about it too much at first—I'm still resting—but by the time the day rolls around when I'm ready to leave, I'm pumped up, excited. I can't wait to get back into the competition. Nothing can hold me back. Roping is what I *do!*"

Leo is not an easy man to live with or travel with. He has little time for those he feels are not as dedicated as he is to rodeo. The Lion has mellowed somewhat through the years, but still takes pleasure occasionally in needling others. Driving through a town somewhere, Leo might spot a restaurant and casually ask his traveling companion, "Would you like to stop here for something to eat?" To which the companion may reply, "Oh, it doesn't matter." That's all Leo needs.

"What do you mean it doesn't matter?" he'll demand. "Of course it matters. Everything matters—that's what life is all about." And then he'll expound on his philosophy of living and winning.

"I must have a real sadistic streak in me," he says, shaking his head.

He was driving out of the big OS Ranch roping near Post, Tex., one year, enroute to another rodeo, and team roper Mike Beers was traveling with him. Leo drives like a demon

He views his rest as a reward, if he has won.

under normal circumstances, but this day he was running a little late. He took a curve on the dirt road at a fairly high rate of speed (he wasn't pulling a trailer), and the pickup did a 360-degree spin, straightened out, and continued down the road. Mike was pale.

"This road's a little rough," said Leo, casually." Maybe you'd better buckle your seat belt." Mike buckled his seat belt. Leo was laughing inside, but never cracked a smile.

Life in the fast lane—it's hard on men and horses, not to mention pickups, and sometimes Leo wonders if the hectic pace is reaching a point of diminishing returns. "Athletes on athletic horses, that's what it is," he says. "I was fortunate to grow up on a ranch, where I learned about the heritage of roping and rodeo. There is logic to what we do in the arena, especially in team roping. So many modern contestants have missed out on this.

"There aren't many famous old rope horses today like there were years ago—the horses aren't around that long. They are being pushed to excel beyond their endurance, and many of them blow up and quit working in less than a year. What a waste. I've got too

With his heeling horses, Stick (left) and Shorty.

much respect for my horses to do that to them."

Leo's horse Stick has been around. The old veteran has seen a lot of country and been with Leo through good times and bad. He survived a trailer wreck in 1975 on the outskirts of Oklahoma City, on the way to the National Finals. The hitch somehow came loose, and Leo watched in horror, in his rearview mirror, as the trailer went off the side of the road and rolled. Leo stopped and raced back to the trailer, fearing the worst. He got Stick free of the wreckage, and the horse stood calmly, then began to graze along the median.

"I knew right then what our partnership meant to me. I felt bad, because I'd let the horse down. It was a miracle he survived, and he wasn't even injured seriously. He just thought it was a rough spot in the road."

The horse was named the year he showed up near the end of the Finals in 1971—at a time when Leo was in need of a new mount. Leo's horse Colorado had become lame late in the season,

and he was using a new horse he had bought; but the new horse wasn't working too well. One of Leo's roping students, a school teacher in South Dakota, was coming to watch the last weekend of the Finals, so Leo asked him to bring along his horse. The gelding had a shaggy mane and feet that needed trimming. One of the cowboys asked The Lion where he got "that stick horse"—and the name stuck.

"He wasn't much to look at when they unloaded him, but he really came alive when I backed him in that box," smiles Leo. "I knew he was special." Leo won the last go-round at the NFR that year, riding Stick. When the time was announced, he took off his hat and threw it to the crowd. Stick is semi-retired now, but still "comes alive" whenever it's time to rope.

Stick is a registered Quarter Horse, whose official name is Keota Van Dee. He was foaled in Mountain Home, Ida., on March 24, 1966. Leo bought Stick but never bothered to transfer his registration papers.

A good horse is important, but there

Sharon and Leo.

is more to life than riding and roping, winning and losing. For Leo there is Sharon, his wife and partner, the only person in the world who can argue with The Lion and come away unscathed. Sharon Meffan was raised in Los Angeles and has had a long-time interest in horses and rodeo. When she was two years old her father started taking her to Redondo Beach every Saturday for pony rides. Summers were spent in the mountains, and as Sharon grew she managed to find nearby mountain pack stations that would give her riding privileges in exchange for work.

When Sharon was about 14, a girlfriend's family bought a livestock sales yard—Sharon spent nearly every weekend at the yard, clear through high school. The girls would help move cattle in and out of the ring, "and tried to make a barrel horse out of every sale horse that came through," she remembers.

Her father took her to watch the National Finals Rodeo in 1964, when it was held in Los Angeles, and Sharon was "really hooked on horses and rodeo after that." She practiced goat tying and breakaway roping as well as barrel racing. Her friend's father finally gave the girls an aged barrel horse named Walter, and Sharon found it feasible to take Walter to college. She went to Pierce Junior College in Woodland Hills on a rodeo scholarship from 1966 through '68, then transferred to Cal Poly at San Luis Obispo, and was graduated with a degree in business management in 1970, the year she won the national intercollegiate rodeo title in goat tying.

Sharon went to work in the spring of 1971 as a flight attendant. She bought a hot-blooded barrel horse to compete on weekends in the Women's Professional Rodeo Association, and this arrangement suited her until 1974, the year she met Leo. "Our first date was a catastrophe," she says. "We butted heads on opinions, and Leo took me home right after dinner. But I was still intrigued with him, so the next day I called him up and suggested he take me to lunch; we got along fine. That was

135

There is pressure on a
header when Leo tells
him at the outset: "All
you have to do is
catch."

in February, and we were married in
November."

Sharon and Leo are compatible competitors, but there are certain strains
placed on the relationship when they
rodeo together. "Leo is pretty good to
travel with, except that he's so fast — he
eats fast, drives fast, sleeps fast . . . and
that wears on your nerves," says
Sharon. "And if you ever get in a
slump, where you're not winning, you
won't get any sympathy from him. He's
hard on himself when he doesn't win,
and that's how he treats others rodeoing with him when they don't win.
He'll build you up by tearing you down
first; you'll get so mad at him that you
try extra hard just to show him, just to
get back at him. Then, after you've ex-
celled, you realize what he was doing. I
understand this, and most seasoned
competitors can see it, too. But a
rookie takes severe criticism pretty
hard."

It's no secret that Leo has schooled
many rookies through the years — he is
always looking for the perfect header.
Some of them, like Dee Pickett and
Tee Woolman, achieved overnight success working with Leo, then struck out
on their own. Others, those no one
hears about, drop by the wayside
quickly — they can't take the strain. Leo
is famous as a heeler, yet he is equally
adept at heading; at a rodeo in 1981 he
headed for this brother Jerold, and the
team won second. There is pressure on
a rookie header who backs in the box,
realizing that his partner may know
more about heading than he does.
There is pressure on a header when Leo

tells him at the outset: "All you have to
do is catch. I'll take care of business;
I'll get us to the rodeos. You don't have
to worry about anything but making
head catches. And if you make enough
catches, you'll have a chance to win a
world championship."

Therein lies the thorn: the opportunity he offers is so simple it becomes
difficult. The rookie thinks, "I *must*
catch." Or, if he does find success according to the terms, he will declare in-
dependence eventually, human nature
being what it is.

Even though Leo has spurred Sharon
on to greater achievements, most of her
success in barrel racing has been
achieved on her own terms; she is a
capable horsewoman and trainer. In
1974 she turned Leo's calf roping horse,
Charlie, into a barrel horse, and made
it to the top 20 in barrel racing. She
bought a young horse named Seven, of
Bar Fifty Cat breeding (who goes back
to Hollywood Gold), and out of a Joe
Reed mare, worked with the horse
several years and cracked him out in
1978 to win the Sierra Circuit in barrel
racing. She won first in the circuit the
following year, and also qualified for
her first National Finals. She made it to
the Finals again in 1980 and '81.

*Most of Sharon's success in barrel racing has
been achieved on her own terms.*

There are unexpected advantages to rodeoing with Sharon, Leo admits.

There are unexpected advantages to traveling with Sharon, Leo admits. Sharon has signed for more than a few speeding tickets in California that Leo incurred. The rig will still be moving when Leo gives the signal for Sharon to scoot across his lap and take the wheel while he moves to the side. "Leo doesn't need any more points on his license," she explains.

The two of them travel together often unless, early in the season after a few big wins, Leo decides to go all out for another shot at the title. When that happens, Sharon will set a more leisurely pace, rodeoing with other barrel racers. She likes to compete in rodeo towns with good restaurants and antique shops, preferably in the Northwest where the climate is relatively cool during summer. She may miss Leo, but she doesn't miss the speeding or hectic schedules.

Sharon is also an accomplished writer and photographer. She used her camera to chronicle the year Leo and Tee Woolman won first at the National Finals, and the result was a professional slide show set to music, a special project for a photography course she took. The class was asked to critique her show, and one student said he felt the program should have ended with the climax, at the National Finals, rather than continuing into more action slides.

The Lion was in the audience, and he stood to speak: "No, the climax should not come at the end, because rodeo isn't like that." He explained how the sport is held year-round, how a new season is actually underway before the previous season closes. Cowboys and championships come and go, he told them, but rodeo has no end. . . .

Fall is a pleasant time of year in central California. The weather is mild; foggy mornings turn into clear days. There is some rain, but the real wet season won't come until winter. Fall is a perfect time to rope.

After the Grand National in San Francisco, the last big contest before the National Finals, Leo will relax around home for a few days, then go to a rodeo or roping the following weekend. But for the next four weeks he will stay fairly close to the house as he undergoes an intense, self-inflicted physical conditioning program.

He rises each day at 6 a.m., feeds horses, then dons jogging shoes and sweatsuit for a five-mile run. Afterwards, he does calisthenics. He showers and changes clothes, skips breakfast, and walks to the stable to ready his

Thoughts of competition have re-kindled the spirit of aggression.

horses for another day of roping. This regimen is usually interrupted briefly when Leo catches a plane to Oklahoma City to show a rope horse for someone at the World Championship Quarter Horse Show, but then it's back to California for more conditioning, more practice. The anticipation grows, and The Lion feels strong.

A week before the Finals, Leo and Sharon load horses and luggage, and start on the long drive to Oklahoma City and the Finals. They feel relaxed and happy — the drive is actually a time of rest for them — and they usually follow the same route each year: to Phoenix the first day, then to El Paso, then to Fort Worth and on to Oklahoma City. Leo's personality is changing by the time they leave Fort Worth on the last leg of the journey. There is little conversation inside the pickup this day, and his eyes are fixed on the highway as his foot presses the accelerator. Thoughts of competition have re-kindled the spirit of aggression. Such is the nature of lions.

— *Randy Witte*

ACKNOWLEDGEMENT

I would like to thank Randy Witte, one of the few writers in my career who has taken the time to ask the questions that led to the recording of my deepest motivations and the driving force that lies behind my competitive spirit.

Also, thanks to Kurt Markus for his willingness to photograph the roping technique I have dedicated my life to achieve.

R U L E S

You've got to know the rules before you compete.

Synopsis of rules from Professional Rodeo Cowboys Association rule book. Check the current PRCA book each year for additional related rules, and for any changes that may be made in rules.

Contestants will start from behind a barrier. In all indoor rodeos header must start from steer wrestling box. There will be a 10-second penalty assessed for breaking or beating the barrier. Animal belongs to contestant when he calls for him, except in cases of mechanical failure, animal escaping arena, and/or fouls. Team roper behind barrier must throw first loop at head.

Each contestant will be allowed to carry but one rope. Each team allowed three throws in all. Roping steers without turning loose the loop will be considered no catch. Roper must dally to stop steer. No tied ropes allowed unless Tie-Face-Option has been approved by team roping director. . . . The option to tie a rope can only be used by those contestants 50 years of age or older and only will be granted at specific rodeos as approved and advised as such.

Time will be taken when steer is roped, both horses facing steer in line with ropes dallied and tight. Horses' front feet must be on ground and ropers must be mounted when time is taken. Steer must be standing up when roped by head or heels. . . .

Steer must not be handled roughly at any time, and ropers may be disqualified if in the opinion of the field judge they have intentionally done so.

If in the opinion of the field flagger a heel loop is thrown before the header has dallied and changed the direction of a steer, team shall be disqualified.

Broken rope or dropped rope will be

considered no time, regardless whether time has been taken or not. . . .

If steer is roped by one horn, roper is not allowed to ride up and put rope over other horn or head with his hands.

If the heeler ropes a front foot or feet in the heel loop, this is a foul catch. Neither contestant may remove the front foot or feet from the loop by hand. However, should the front foot or feet come out of the heel loop by the time the field flag judge drops his flag, time will be counted. . . .

There shall be two timers, a barrier judge, and a field flag judge. Time to be taken between two flags.

The length of score will be determined by arena conditions. The minimum length of score at all rodeos will be the length of the roping box minus four (4) feet. All score lengths are subject to team roping director or representative approval. . . .

Legal Catches. There will be only three legal head catches:

1. Around both horns.
2. Half a head.
3. Around the neck.

If honda passes over one horn and the loop over the other, catch is illegal.

One hind foot receives 5-second fine.

If loop crosses itself in a head catch, it is illegal. This does not include heel catches.

Printed with permission of: Professional Rodeo Cowboys Association, 101 Prorodeo Drive, Colorado Springs, CO 80919

TERMINOLOGY

Rodeo and team roping parlance.

AVERAGE — Competitions with more than one go-round pay prize money for each round, plus money for the best average, or total time. The winner of the average is the overall winner of the contest.

BARRIER — The rope that is stretched across the front of the box from which the header emerges. If the header rides through the rope and breaks the barrier before the steer has tripped the release mechanism, the team receives a ten-second penalty. The Hallettsville automatic barrier is the most popular in use.

BOX — The area along the side of the chute, where horse and rider stand, ready to rope. Most arenas have a box on either side of the chute, one for the header and one for the heeler, but some arenas have just one large box, from which both ropers emerge for the competition.

BURNER — The small piece of leather laced on the honda of a rope to prevent the honda from wearing out.

CHUTE — The small enclosure from which the steer is released into the arena.

CURL — Refers to the upward curling action of a loop as it encircles horns or heels. A good curl indicates the loop has been thrown well.

DALLY — The process of wrapping the tail of the rope around the saddle horn, counter-clockwise at least once, after the loop has caught a steer around the head or heels. The dally will hold or stop the steer.

DIAMETER — In reference to a rope, this is the width or thickness of a rope, ranging from 5/16ths to 7/16ths of an inch. The most popular ropes are 3/8ths and 7/16ths.

ENTRY FEE — The amount of money a contestant pays to enter a competition. Entry fees are pooled to form prize money. At all PRCA rodeos, and some individual ropings, the fees are also added to purse money to form total prize money. At some ropings, a "stock charge" is taken out of the fees before pooling, to pay for the use of the steers.

FACE UP — After the heeler has made his catch and dallied, the header turns his horse to face the heeler with both ropes taut, steer in the middle, and this signals the end of the run.

FIGURE-EIGHT HEAD CATCH — One of the most common illegal head catches, when the loop crosses itself between the horns, forming a figure-eight. With an illegal catch, a team is "flagged out" and receives "no time."

GO-ROUND — Also referred to as "round." A competition will have at least one go-round; a go-round is complete when every contestant has competed once.

HEADER — The team roping partner who throws the first loop, at the steer's horns. The three legal head catches are: "clean horn catch" (when the loop settles perfectly around both horns), "half-head catch" (when the loop settles around the steer's head, under his jaw, and encircles one horn), and "around the neck" (when the loop settles around the steer's neck). All other head catches are illegal.

HEELER — The team roping partner who throws the second loop, at the heels. There are no restrictions on heel catches as long as the loop actually encircles both heels. If only one heel is caught, a five-second penalty is assessed.

HONDA — The eye in one end of the rope. The other end of the rope is passed through the honda to form a loop.

JACKPOT — A competition in which only entry fees are pooled for prize money. No purse money is added. A "drawpot" is run under the same conditions, but contestants draw for partners, and the steers are loaded into the chute randomly.

JERK — Refers to the abrupt contact by means of the rope between heading horse and steer when the steer is initially stopped by the header.

LAP-AND-TAP — A roping competition that is run without using a barrier.

LAY — In reference to a rope, the lay is the stiffness factor of a particular rope, ranging from soft to hard.

LOGGING — The term used for pulling, when a horse pulls a steer (or some weighted object during training) with a rope dallied to the saddle horn.

NECK ROPE — In reference to a steer, this is the loop placed around a steer's neck in the chute. The other end of the rope triggers release of the barrier when the steer reaches the scoreline; at the same time, a piece of string connecting the loop around the steer's neck breaks free, removing the loop from the steer.

PULLING SLACK — The act of grasping the rope with a hand after the loop has settled on the target, and pulling, thereby taking the "slack" out of the rope and tightening the loop. Synonymous terms include "grabbing slack" or "jerking slack," but the action is more of a strong fluid pull, rather than an abrupt jerk on the rope.

RATE — A good roping horse should rate cattle to afford the rider the best throw. A horse does this by moving into the correct position behind the steer, and maintaining an even speed with the steer while the rider swings his loop and prepares to throw.

SCORE — This word has a couple of meanings, according to the context in which it is used. It may refer to the length of head start given a steer from the chute to the scoreline (perhaps 8 to 15 feet or more, depending on individual arena conditions). Or it may refer to the horse training procedure whereby the horse is held in the box while a steer is released from the chute, but the roper prevents the horse from pursuing the steer. This teaches the horse not to anticipate, and to leave the box only when the roper signals him to leave. A good rope horse should "score well."

SPOKE — The section or length of rope not in the loop, but held next to the loop, between the honda and the roper's hand.

THE "L" — This is the general angle (90 degrees) in which a team roping run takes place. The angle is formed when the header ropes and dallies, then pulls the steer across the arena enabling the heeler to make his catch.

WRAPPING THE HORN — For dally roping, it's best to wrap the saddle horn with something to protect it from rope wear, and to help keep the dally from slipping. Many ropers prefer to cross-cut an old innertube, slicing off a big "rubberband" that is two or three inches thick. The rubber is then looped and wound around the saddle horn until it is stretched tight.

WRAPPING STEERS' HORNS — This refers to the protective coverings attached to the base of a steer's horns, to prevent rope burns on the animal when he is headed. The best wraps are usually made of leather, and may be purchased at many saddle shops, or rodeo equipment stores.

Western Horseman Magazine

Editorial & Advertising Offices
Colorado Springs, Colorado

The Western Horseman Magazine, established in 1936, is the world's leading horse publication. For subscription information, write: Western Horseman Magazine, P.O. Box 7980, Colorado Springs, Colorado 80933.